LIGHTING THE WAY

HOW KIRISM ANSWERS LIFE'S TOUGHEST QUESTIONS

ERIC MAISEL

CROSSWAYS PRESS

Eric Maisel, Ph.D.

** for Ann **

Created with Vellum

PREFACE

This volume is an introduction to the philosophy of kirism.

Kirism is a contemporary philosophy of life that I've been developing over the past several years. It has its roots in many soils—existentialism, stoicism, language analysis, deconstructive postmodernism, philosophy of science, and social psychology among them—and takes an ordinary-language approach to the main questions that any philosophy of life must address, among them "What is life all about?" and "How shall I live?"

Often without quite knowing it, human beings crave a philosophy of life. Typically, they embrace a philosophy or religion for a period of time and find something worthy in it and also lots with which they disagree. Over time, they grow in the belief that their chosen philosophy or religion doesn't match their understanding of the nature of reality, nor does it speak to how they would like to live.

Life purpose and meaning issues remain, basic questions about what to do, where to turn, and why to do anything persist, dark, unsettling feelings circulate in their system, and the thing commonly called "depression" descends. Anxiety is experienced as a constant companion and life feels chaotic, meager, and unlived. Can any philosophy of life make a real difference with any of that? I believe that kirism can.

A philosophy of life that makes sense to you can make all the difference in the world. I believe that kirism will make sense to you. When you acquaint yourself with the difference between life purpose and life purposes, with the value of self-authorship and self-obligation, and with the other ideas of kirism, you will find yourself calmed by your new understanding and clear about how to proceed with life.

Kirism attempts to describe the nature of human reality and suggests how a person might want to live so as to have his life match his best intentions. It asserts that a person can have the experience of his life mattering, even if the universe is indifferent, even if life's obstacles are relentless and enduring, and even if his own personality is an obstacle. If a single sentence could describe kirism, it would be: "Kirism tries to describe the nature of human reality and paint a picture of how we can best live."

Kirism may speak to you. If it does, you might wonder, how can I be a part of this? The answer is: by living as a kirist. In the future, there may be kirist gatherings and other ways that kirists meet one another, communicate with one another, join in common causes and create shared experiences. But, even if that were to happen, the primary way for you to be a part of kirism is by living life as a kirist. That will serve you; and that will also serve us all.

Please enjoy this volume. I hope it serves you and makes a difference in your life.

1

BOOK I. INTRODUCING KIRISM

1. A philosophy of life is an attempt at a comprehensive answer to the question, "How shall I live as a human being?" It is an attempt at a big answer to a big question. Kirism, which I have developed, is a contemporary attempt at that big answer.

2. Any such answer should not be imposed upon you. It should be of your own choosing. It shouldn't be your parents, your church, your community, or your government ordering your allegiance. Your philosophy of life should be your own.

3. Kirism demands no allegiance. It presents some ideas and makes some suggestions but has no commandments. It wonders aloud, "What do you think?" If you agree with its ideas, then you nod. If you disagree, then you shake your head.

4. But do you even need a philosophy of life? That must be a first question. Can't you just wake up, brush your teeth, hop on the bus, go off to work, shuffle papers, come on

home, and watch a show? Isn't life straightforward and easy like that?

5. To a kirist, probably not. If you are reading this, you probably require more from yourself than just going through some repetitive motions. You know that when you just go through the motions, life feels meaningless, empty, and disappointing.

6. A useful philosophy of life ought to help you do more than just go through the motions. It should paint a picture of the world as it is, including the worlds of consciousness and mind, and make suggestions that strike you as valuable and true.

7. Past philosophies and religions have not done an excellent job on either score, either with regard to accurately describing the world or with regard to making suggestions that sound and feel true. That is why a new, updated philosophy is needed.

8. Any useful contemporary philosophy of life should have an historical sense and incorporate an understanding of the last five hundred years of human activity, chronicling how we have arrived at our current sense of meaning—and meaninglessness.

9. Starting in the seventeenth century, we experienced four hundred years of the celebration—and inflation—of the individual. Certain amazing ideas bloomed and some even more amazing realities followed. We got individual rights!

10. We got the sense that man might get to know himself and his world. We got scientific and technological progress on all fronts. There we were, beating back disease and living long lives. A wild, strange euphoria arose: man mattered!

11. But disaster was brewing. We pushed the curtain back and stood face-to-face with a reality so cold that the space between the stars seemed blazing hot by comparison. Science, unintentionally and without malice, knocked us down a peg.

12. And holocausts continued. People still starved. With nuclear weapons came our ability to extinguish the species in the blink of an eye. Man, for all his supposed progress and grand enlightenment, dropped a huge notch in his own estimation.

13. The more that we announced that man mattered, the more that we saw that he really didn't. The better we understood that the dinosaurs could be extinguished by an asteroid strike, the better we understood our own individual fate.

14. The better we understood the power of microbes, and even as we worked hard to fight them, the better we understood that something invisible and endlessly prevalent could end our personal journey on any given afternoon. Boom!

15. The more science taught us, the more we shrank in size—and shrank back in horror. You could build the largest particle accelerator the world had ever seen and recreate the Big Bang—and, psychologically speaking, end up with only more of nothing.

16. Even more of nothing. And this is where we are today; and this is what a kirist faces. We had somehow wagered that well-stocked supermarkets and guaranteed elections would do the trick and protect us from the void. They haven't. This we face.

17. This now shared certainty that we are throwaways has

made life look completely unfunny. We can laugh and make small talk but in most of our private moments there is not much laughter. There is only a deep, wide, abiding "Why bother?"

18. Kirists answer that question in the following way: "While we are here, we have the self-obligation to bother and the self-obligation to act as if we matter, a mattering that includes acting ethically and putting the whole world on our shoulders."

19. To accomplish this, you take as much control as possible of your thoughts, your attitudes, your moods, your behaviors, and your very orientation toward life and you make use of the freedom you possess in the service of your noblest intentions.

20. You identify your life purposes and take responsibility for your life purpose choices, you deal with meaninglessness by making daily meaning investments and by seizing daily meaning opportunities, and you dismiss absurdity as true but irrelevant.

21. I've given these various connected ideas a name: kirism. Kirism focuses on adamant personal responsibility set against a backdrop of cosmic indifference. It endeavors to be wise about human nature, psychological reality, and the world we live in.

22. Why the name 'kirism'? Because 'kirism' has many charming associations. The Slavic and Romany word for 'inn' is 'kir 'c 'ima.' You might think of kirism as an inn for existential travelers, a waystation where we cross paths for an evening.

23. In Sumerian 'kara' means 'to shine' and 'kar' means 'to illuminate.' 'Szikra' means 'spark' in Hungarian, 'gira'

means 'fire' in the African dialect of East Cushitic, and 'iskra' means 'sparkle' in Serbo-Croatian. Aren't those lovely associations?

24. But, really, what's in a name? What matters is what kirism stands for. It stands for radical goodness, radical self-obligation and radical individualism. It stands for self-awareness, powerful self-determination, intentional living and absurd rebellion.

25. Kirists take personal responsibility. Personal responsibility is our north star. Radical goodness is its twin, shining equally brightly. If we live that way, acting ethically and living a life of purpose, we'll likely also be gifted with experiences of meaning.

26. Kirism asserts that, like it or not, we have been forced into the role of steward and arbiter of our life. Surely no one asked for that. Who wouldn't prefer an orgasm, a tidy income, a little selfishness, and another round of golf? Wouldn't you?

27. Kirists can't live that way because we know that we ought not to live that way. There is not an ounce of goodness in that picture. There is only comfort, pleasure, and privilege. It is quite the charming picture but it doesn't work for an ethical being.

28. Kirists can't take that easy route. We say, "I expect no occult payoffs from acting ethically, no nirvana, no heaven, no enlightenment, no Nobel Prizes of the soul. There is only my life as project, with some self-respect as the main payoff."

29. One Saturday morning I am writing in a small neighborhood park in Paris. The park is full. On a nearby bench, a woman is angry with a man. He tries to mollify

her. On the next bench sit a middle-aged couple who have no need to say anything.

30. Near me are two old women, one sprightlier than the other and annoyed at her friend's decrepitude. Outside the park's swinging gates a seated woman holding an infant is begging. Around me, a dozen boys are sword-fighting.

31. This is our species. This is life: concrete, real, and various. Everything human is here. Kirists aspire to accept this variety, this concreteness, this reality. Might it be lovely to be another sort of creature with another destiny? But this is who we are.

32. Kirism is an aspirational philosophy. We aspire to do a better job than average of manifesting our values, minding our thoughts, and living our life purposes. We do this not to pass some universal test but to live as we know we ought to live.

33. Inside our cocoon of psychological subjectivity, a cocoon that makes it hard to see clearly, we aspire to self-awareness. That is another absurdity that we accept as a given. How can such a subjective creature possibly see objectively? But we try!

34. We try. We can't escape our psychological subjectivity, as we are embedded inside of it. But we can wonder about our motives, make guesses about our intentions, and speculate about where we may be fooling ourselves. We can reflect.

35. As we reflect, we are likely to come to the following conclusions about living. What follows are some of the main suggestions of kirism. These suggestions, presented here are headlines, are elaborated in the other books in this volume.

36. *Kirists actively identify their life purposes.* They decide what's important to them. This sounds obvious enough as a sensible thing to do but few people do it. Most people miss this opportunity at self-creation, for all sorts of reasons.

37. A primary reason is that they've been taught that life has "a purpose." As a result, they keep hunting unsuccessfully for that singular purpose. But life has no singular purpose. It is made up of the life purpose choices that a human being champions.

38. *Kirists live their life purposes.* This sounds obvious enough. If you knew what your life purposes were, surely you would want to live them. But even people who have a good sense of what their life purposes are have difficulty actually living them.

39. This is because tasks, chores, errands, and everything else is allowed to come first; because juggling multiple life purposes is difficult; and because living our life purposes requires rather more effort than, say, napping or turning on the television.

40. *Kirists organize life around their life purposes.* When they wake up, kirists hear themselves say, "What are the important things?" Not, "What do I have to get done?" or "What did I leave undone?" but "What are the important things?"

41. These important things might include having that hard conversation with your son about his drinking, making a sharp political statement, or creating your online business. Every day, you tackle as many of these important things as you can.

42. *Kirists live as if they matter.* The contemporary person has powerful reasons for believing that he or she doesn't matter. But kirists reject that simply because we may be the

product of an indifferent universe, we shouldn't act as if we matter.

43. We matter by living our life purposes, by acting ethically, and, absurdly enough, by taking responsibility for keeping civilization afloat. This is self-obligation, ordered by no one and ratified by no one, and the primary way that we make ourselves proud.

44. *Kirists live ethically*. We live in a time when that stalwart phrase from the 19th century, "truth, beauty and goodness," has been shredded by the analytical knives of linguistic philosophy. Today, it is hard to utter that phrase with a straight face.

45. Yet we are obliged to circle back around to innocence and to stand up for goodness, even though we know that badness is often rewarded, even though we know that our values compete and clash, and even in the absence of absolute moral principles.

46. *Kirists retain their individuality*. Many forces within the family and society will attempt to constrain you and limit you by bullying you, shaming you, hurling insults, invoking arbitrary rules, and employing every manner of violence and meanness.

47. You may be silenced and made to feel small in subtle ways or you may be told flat-out that you do not count, that you will never amount to anything, that you had better fit in and listen or else. A kirists fights against this subjugation her whole life.

48. *Kirists aim for meaning without craving it*. The experience of meaning is just that, a certain sort of experience. We can work to have more such experiences: we can try to coax

meaning into existence. But we shouldn't pine too much for meaning.

49. Kirists understand that meaning is merely a certain sort of psychological experience. It comes and it goes; it can't be counted on; it can't be ordered up. Kirists do their best to not crave it a lot and to focus instead on living their life purposes.

50. *Kirists give life a thumb's up.* Without quite realizing it, many people have given up on life. They've made the mental calculation that life has cheated them, that life isn't what it's cracked up to be, that life isn't worth the candle.

51. This conclusion leads to chronic sadness. It makes it hard to stick with things or to believe in your own efforts. Kirists make the conscious decision to give life a thumb's up, even if they have ample reasons to come to a different, harsher conclusion.

52. *Kirists start their day with an intentional practice.* It is unsettling and unsatisfying to rush through life, doing one thing after another and never getting to the things that matter. One strategy? To start your day by doing something that matters.

53. That might be a creativity practice, a health practice, a recovery practice, a business-building practice, an activism practice, a mindfulness practice, a personality upgrade practice: that is, it might be anything that you deem important.

54. Kirism has no set of obligatory practices. But one suggested practice is a morning practice that helps you settle, quiet your nerves, and attend to your life purposes. A daily morning practice can serve as a sure anchor in the turbulent sea of life.

55. *Kirists negotiate each day*. Kirists conceptualize each day as something requiring a high degree of mindful organization. Because what's most important may also be what's hardest, kirists know to pencil in and underline their important tasks.

56. A negotiated day might include an hour devoted to creating, an hour devoted to relating, an hour devoted to activism, many hours of everyday drudgery, and a bit of relaxation. This might amount to a seriously excellent day.

57. *Kirists think thoughts that serve them*. If we are thinking thoughts that reduce our motivation, that make us doubt our abilities, that increase our anxiety, or that plummet us into despair, we have become a weakened version of ourselves.

58. Kirists set the bar very high by demanding of themselves that they only think thoughts that serve them. This means that they bravely hear what they are saying, see through their own tricks, and send unwanted and derailing thoughts packing.

59. *Kirists indwell with awareness*. We see value in the metaphor of "the room that is our mind": the place that we inhabit, that possesses qualities (like airlessness), and that we can redesign (say, by adding windows that let in a breeze).

60. If we don't pay sufficient attention, that "room" can become a place where we relentlessly nag ourselves or talk ourselves into despair. If, instead, we serve as self-architect, it can become a place of calmness, contemplation, and creation.

61. *Kirists upgrade their personality*. We see personality as made up of three constituent parts, original personality (who we

come into the world as), formed personality (who we stiffen into), and available personality (our remaining freedom).

62. Kirists use their available personality to reckon with their original personality and to upgrade their formed personality. In the process, they create more available personality. This simple model helps them remember that they are their primary project.

63. *Kirists deconstruct the idea of work.* Most people are obliged to spend two-thirds of their waking time doing work to pay the bills. Work is a great thief, robbing huge amounts of time and energy. This is as true for kirists as for anyone.

64. Some small percentage of workers love what they do. Some small percentage approach their work with decent equanimity. The vast majority dislike their work or even hate it. Kirists understand the lifelong challenges presented by the need to work.

65. *Kirists recognize the power of psychological entanglements.* Rather than picture emotional difficulties or troublesome behaviors as mental disorders, kirists point to the entangling nature of experience: how experiences live on in the mind and body.

66. Who isn't tangled up with thoughts and feelings about their parents, their siblings, their rivals, their career failures, their regrets, their disappointments? Kirists pay attention to their own psychological entanglements and watch out for them in others.

67. *Kirists recognize that significant tension exists between their humanistic impulses and their selfish genes.* Like all living things, we are self-interested. But nature has also constructed us to conjure with ideas like democracy, justice, and civil rights.

68. This confuses everyone. One second we give to charity. The next second we covet. One second we love our classmate's story. The next second we hate him for winning first prize. Kirists know that no one escapes this particular rollercoaster.

69. *Kirists live as rebels.* If you remain individual, thinking your own thoughts, acting ethically, speaking up as required, and living in the fullness of your life purposes, you are bound not to fit into your society very well. So, you will have to be adamant.

70. You will have to deal with the forces of society that want to constrain you and silence you. Kirists live a life of action and courage as absurd rebels who have decided to matter. They live this life openly and proudly, without embarrassment.

71. *Kirists appreciate subversive intimacy.* Although profoundly alone, kirists understand the value of community, institutions, friendships, and family. They especially cherish intimate relationships. They know that love and a human touch matter.

72. But they need their intimate relationships to work. A too-ordinary relationship, where neither partner really cares for the other, respects the other, or advocates for the other, will not do. Kirists hold out for something more committed and better.

73. This better intimacy has a particular flavor to it. Together the partners create a bastion of safety and sanity in an unsafe world. Their love is subversive, in the sense that a two-person resistance cell hidden away in occupied territory is subversive.

74. The above are some of the ideas and suggestions of

kirism. You'll find many more in the rest of this volume. I hope that you're beginning to see its outline, its intentions, and its basic thrust. And I hope it speaks to you. I have my fingers crossed!

75. Of course, kirism asks a lot. It is a grown-up philosophy of life short on wishful thinking about the beneficence of the universe, our chances in the afterlife, the goodness of our fellow man, or how easy it will be to fulfil our self-obligations.

76. Each day we must decide what matters to us. Each day we are obliged to figure out how to deal with life. Our life is our project and we strive to rise to the occasion. None of this guarantees the experience of meaning; but it definitely helps.

77. Kirism is an ambitious philosophy that demands that human beings try their hardest. It asks them to make use of the freedom they possess, look life in the eye, and stand tall as an advocate for—and as an example of—human dignity.

78. It argues that life relentlessly pairs tremendous ordinariness with tremendous difficulty. In the face of all that, human beings must nevertheless adopt an indomitable attitude and work to coax out the measure of meaning they require.

79. This is not really to most people's taste. It makes work for them; it pesters them to be moral; it demands that they articulate their life purposes and actually live them; and it announces that a kind of perpetual rebellion is necessary.

80. But it is also beautiful. It is a way of life that encourages the best in you. It matches the high-bar vision you have of yourself as an instrumental, creative, ethical

person who thinks for himself, rejects humbug, and puts the world on his shoulders.

81. Kirism may be for you. You may find it reasonable and true-to-life. You may appreciate its humanistic values and its core principles. And you may decide that adopting kirism as your philosophy of life might genuinely serve you. If so, I'm pleased.

82. Ah, but do any card-carrying kirists actually exist? Well, we have no cards to carry. We have no newsletters, no secret handshakes, no annual conferences. So, it's hard to tell. It's likely we just occasionally bump into one another —without knowing it.

83. And remember, kirism is new. We shall see what the future brings. Maybe it will grow. If you embrace it, that increases our numbers by one. If you tell a friend, that might make two. Then maybe someone from Japan will join, and then someone from France ...

84. For now, just do the next right thing. And the right thing after that. Then, there you would be, self-aware, purposeful, aligned with your values, in a sea of shifting meaning, aiming for the good and undaunted by human puniness. That will work!

85. And please do read on. I think you'll find the remaining books in this volume pertinent and interesting. Kirism is a consistent, contemporary, humbug-free, true-to-life philosophy of life that may, at a minimum, interest you; and might really serve you.

2

BOOK II. SELF-OBLIGATION & SELF-AUTHORSHIP

1. Kirists believe in self-obligation and self-authorship. We decide what we deem is important, rooting each decision in an absurd obligation to do the right thing. We accept that we are burdened with freedom and the moral imperative to stand up.

2. This absurd obligation to do right and to live our life purposes presses us into action. If it is storming outside and we have no desire to go out but we are obliged to venture out, then we go, complaining a bit, under the weather a bit, but adamantly.

3. We do not say "What's the point?" or "Who cares?" or "This is too hard!" or "I quit." Or rather, we may say all that, but then we laugh, or at least chuckle a little, and get on with the business of raising our personal bar very high, to self- respect.

4. Our life is our project. We are tasked by no one but ourselves to live a life that makes us proud. Nature has built us to know that this is true and has also built us to be

not quite equal to the task. This project management is hard, but there is no help for that.

5. Self-obligation is the motivation. Self-authorship is the way. This is different from duty. We may see it as our duty to show up for work. But it is our obligation to decide whether our work is righteous or not. If it isn't, that matters.

6. Maybe our work is pastoral. Maybe we've been mouthing platitudes about God for decades. Now we've come to the place of knowing that we do not believe. It may be our duty to preach on Sunday but it is now our obligation to stop that lying.

7. Maybe we grew up in a culture that demands that we honor our ancestors and everyone who is older than us. But our parents happen to be toxic, dangerous tyrants. Our culture may say that it is our duty to submit to them but it is our obligation to rebel.

8. Maybe we see it as our duty to maintain a perfectly tidy house. But we have little children who can't be tidy unless we drown them in rules and discipline them harshly. It is our obligation to change our mind about the supreme importance of neatness.

9. We may have acquired all sorts of ideas about what is correct behavior and right living. But we know better than to believe that those rules are written in stone. For we may have been mistaken, deluded, coerced, misguided or wrong- headed.

10. We are obliged to rethink ourselves and reinvent ourselves as we go. It is not some badge of honor to stick to our guns and refuse to change. How many costly mistakes

will we repeat if we have no permission to examine our unconscious premises?

11. We say, "I intend to do the next right thing and the right thing after that. I am obliged to live that way because I know that matches my vision of how my life ought to be lived. To live that way, I am obliged to bring real attention to every situation."

12. We see life as a series of situations that need our attention. For instance, we may prefer peacefulness to violence. But if we are threatened, we are obliged to decide, in that moment and in that context, whether or not we ought to do violence.

13. In that moment, and in every moment of life, there is no principle or set of principles to rely on except the bedrock principle that we are obliged to do the next right thing. If we do less, we will disappoint ourselves. That is our first principle.

14. But what is the next right thing? Sometimes we know. At other times, we face a muddy picture. We surrender to that reality, that sometimes we feel certain that we know and that at other times we stand agitated, perplexed, and uncertain.

15. This means that we will not always feel certain. A kirist accepts this truth. Others may act as if they are always perfectly certain and that there is no need or place for doubt in their universe. We know that they are only being grandiose and defensive.

16. But, while we may feel uncertain, we still act, and with energy. We make provisional whole-hearted commitments to our choices. We stand up and act bravely, while at the

same time assessing if we've chosen wisely. That is our rhythm and our method.

17. This assessing is essential because our wisdom is regularly threatened by our cravings, our instincts, and our shadowy self-interests. Are we doing the next right thing or just something we want to do? We need to be mindful and watchful.

18. We are genuinely self-interested creatures. Our genes are more than a little selfish. We want what we want. Maybe we want to design ball gowns. Designing ball gowns is bound to make us a puppet of the rich. But how badly we want to design them!

19. Maybe we want to write poetry, even though there are barricades we ought to be storming. Maybe we are committed to one person and find ourselves coveting another. Maybe we are obsessed with trivial amusements. We want what we want!

20. The terrible power of craving, a power so enormous as to make sloths, liars, and traitors out of anyone, must be reckoned with. Nature plunked craving right down beside our consciousness of good and evil and chuckled, "Okay, humans, deal with this."

21. It is an unequal battle. Our instincts, cravings, desires and shadows are no joke. We attempt to meet this challenge by taking an amazing step to the side of our own desires. This one-step dance to the side is the kirist dance of self- awareness.

22. Maybe we desire a mansion. We know that we do not need five thousand square feet of emptiness but still we want it, maybe to heal some wound, maybe to allow us to

exclaim, "I win!" We take a mindful step to the side and unpack that desire.

23. Maybe we want to feel victorious. Nature has built competition right into us. We know it's wrong-headed to miss our child's recital because our home team is playing, but something in our head screams, "Go, Warriors!" We take a step to the side.

24. Maybe we want acclaim. We seriously doubt that acclaim is of value but our heart hungers for it. We want applause and red-carpet moments, even though we know better. We take a mindful step to the side and have a quiet conversation.

25. That kirist step to the side, which creates space and a vantage point, allows for quiet conversations without which ethical action is impossible. If we are always noisy, unruly, and covetous, if we never create quiet, we'll act from the shadows.

26. How much better to step to the side and reflect. It is such an effortless dance, so much easier, really, than memorizing rules provided by strangers or acting impulsively and making a mess that then needs cleaning up. It's just a single step to the side.

27. Maybe you don't want to notice how meaningless life feels. You're terrified that if you notice you'll invite despair. But aren't you despairing already? Take that quiet step to the side, breathe, and say, "How can I coax some more meaning?"

28. There, off to the side of all that noise, off to the side of all that anxiety and self-pestering, you honor your obligation to listen to your own wisdom and you make quiet deci-

sions about your life purposes and the next steps of your journey.

29. This is an aspect of self-obligation, to step to one side and thoughtfully consider. You know that you are obliged to do this. It is likewise an aspect of self-authorship. From this vantage point, off to one side, you make considered decisions.

30. Maybe you don't want to do battle with your own personality. You rather like your dramas, your messes, and your rages. But you know better. You step to one side, smile wryly at your petulant immaturities, and author a better you.

31. Maybe you've invested two decades in a career that now holds no meaning for you. You could swallow hard and try not to notice that you are miserable. Instead, you step to one side, take several deep breaths, and begin to write a new story.

32. Maybe one of your children is bullying the other. You could shake your head and call it a phase. You could argue that the bullied child will be toughened up by the experience. You could do nothing. Instead, you step to one side and say, "I'm obliged here."

33. The kirist vantage point is off to one side, reflecting on the situation. This helps us not join mobs, not sit entranced by mass culture, and not dive into shallow enthusiasms. Off to one side, we calmly and quietly assess the situation.

34. From that vantage point, we do battle with those powerful impulses that cause us to race around town chasing a high, an orgasm, a sale, or some other excitement. In that quiet place, we make thoughtful choices that amount to self-authorship.

35. From that vantage point, we make our wisest choices. We may not be certain and doubts may remain, but at least we've done our due diligence, thoughtfully considering the matter. We may still want what we want but we act from a higher obligation.

36. Yes, we really do want what we want. Still, we manage to announce, "Self-obligation comes first." Our selfish genes may want mansions but we say, loud enough so that we can hear ourselves, "More righteousness and less square footage."

37. Self-obligation is not the same as self-control. They sound similar but self-control is a whole-body tightness and self-obligation is the breathtaking freedom to do the next right thing. They are as different as handcuffs and goodness.

38. Self-obligation is not the same as self-interest. Self-interest is our greedy self. Self-obligation is our ethical self. Sometimes there is not an inch of difference between them. But often there is a mile of difference between them.

39. Self-obligation is not the same as self-absorption. We do not step to one side to star gaze, to navel gaze, to fantasize, or to lose ourselves in reveries. We step to one side so as to make decisions about what is right and how we shall live.

40. Self-obligation sounds stern. But it is actually happiness for a creature like us, one burdened with a consciousness of good and evil. You are made happy by righteousness. It is not the same happiness as eating ice cream; it is subtler and higher.

41. And self-authorship? Self-authorship requires that you accept how authorship really works. Authorship means a

radical acceptance of messy process. You go into the unknown and you learn as you go. Your first draft may need the ashcan. So be it!

42. Your story is bound to shift. Yesterday it may have been your truth that you did not want children. Today it may be your truth that you do want children. Your story has a new plot line. Kirists grow easy with the shifting storylines of life.

43. Your story may shift this way. Twenty years ago, the idea of being a psychiatrist seemed exactly right. You went to medical school and built your practice. Today, you despise pushing pills as a cure for life's challenges. Your story has a new plot line!

44. Your story may shift this way. You were a brooding teenager and a reckless twenty-something. At thirty, despair took over. You look back, shake your head, and smile. Now you're a kirist. Your story has shifted from author-less to authored.

45. The creative process comes with mistakes, messes, changes of heart, changes of direction, occasional inspiration, and a lot of not knowing. The same for the process of life. You author your life like a creator wrestling an alligator.

46. What might stand in the way of self-authorship? Maybe never having the idea pop into your head. Maybe you were already indoctrinated by age nine or felt defeated by age twelve and never heard yourself say, "My life is entirely mine to direct."

47.What might stand in the way? Your clan. Your clan will certainly reject your efforts at self-authorship. They have been subtly or overtly telling you who you're supposed to be and how you're supposed to act since birth and they are no doubt telling you still.

48.Your peers will certainly reject your efforts at self-authorship. Each of them enters a system that makes demands, including the demand of strict loyalty, and if you say, as a matter of self-authorship, "Your system is flawed," they will despise you.

49. The world's thieves and bullies will certainly reject your efforts at self-authorship. They love freedom for themselves and hate freedom for you. Their goals are to control you, diminish you, and ridicule you, not applaud your thoughtful, singular journey.

50. Your religion or philosophy will almost certainly reject your efforts at self-authorship, unless it is unusually benign and enlightened. As a rule, you will be instructed to follow, not lead, and to accept their dogma as the gospel truth.

51. Your employer will almost certainly reject your efforts at self-authorship. He will demand loyalty, secrecy, subservience, obedience, and lots of company cheerleading. You are to toe the line at all times, not venture out and write your own script.

52. All these forces and many others stand opposed to your efforts at self-authorship. And you yourself may be opposed to the idea. You may hate carrying the weight of freedom on your shoulders and happily drop it for the sake of a certain ease.

53. You may find it less stressful, more convenient, altogether safer and maybe even more responsible to wear blinders, nod in agreement, bow to every pressure, and never stand up or speak up. Of course, this won't make you feel very proud.

54. In our philosophy, you are obliged to thoughtfully author your own life, aiming to do as much good as possible, because your ethical sense demands that. Have you had a recent chat with yourself in which you lay out those obligations?

55. Maybe you once had that chat with yourself on a train ride from Budapest to Vienna or maybe you had it a very long time ago, when you were four years old, as you listened to a fairy tale about good and evil. But have you had it recently?

56. Have it now, again or the first time. This chat sounds like the following. "Hello, me. I guess I am writing my own story. This makes me feel very uncomfortable. This puts a lot of pressure on me to be calm, thoughtful, wise and good. But I'm obliged!"

57. Self-authorship means tolerating the process of life, just as a creator must tolerate the creative process. A creator knows that no creation comes with a guarantee of excellence or a certificate of meaning. You make the effort and then you see.

58. You make the effort. Self-authorship is effortful. You may hear yourself murmur "I'd like to take it easy" or "I prefer a little drama to all this steadiness!" But you catch yourself. You remind yourself that self-authorship is exactly this demanding.

59. Kirism is demanding. You can certainly find philosophies and religions that demand much less, or even nothing. There are plenty of breezy philosophies and religions that do not ask you to do much, be much, or care much. Are they for you?

60. You can also find plenty of philosophies and religions

that demand a lot, much more than kirism does, but with all that demanding coming from on high. Most philosophies and religions are like that, full of dogma delivered by iron fists.

61. You can find all sorts of philosophies and religions that boss you about, that meddle in every corner of your life, that have you bowing and scraping, that tell you what to wear, what to eat, what to think and which way to face. Are they for you?

62. Kirism is demanding but it only makes proper demands that match your understanding of what's required. You yourself appoint yourself an ordinary hard worker in the service of justice and goodness. You demand that of yourself.

63. Among those appropriate demands are steadiness and a serial letting go. You stay steady in your determination to author your story and to meet your self-obligations. At the same time, when change must occur you let go of your desire to cling.

64. When must you let go? You could jump high when you were twenty and now you can barely get off the ground. So be it. You organize your life around your new reality and you do not sign up for any high hurdle races, despite the temptation.

65. When must you let go? Your career made sense to you a decade ago. Now it doesn't. Maybe you can make new sense of it, maybe you can wait it out to retirement, or maybe you are obliged to make a huge change. You decide without clinging.

66. When must you let go? You hoped that your children would have children. They have their own ideas. If you

cling to that hope you will only create pain and resentment. You let go of your demanding desire and love your children as they are.

67. Where must you stay steady? You stay steady in the knowledge that the universe has no messages for you and no secret missions for you. You accept that the locus of purpose is within you, not out there somewhere in the vast reaches of darkness.

68. Where must you stay steady? You stay steady in your belief that you are obliged to live your life in a worthy way. You have chosen this obligation and ratified your choice. This is bedrock, though when the rains come it can get slippery.

69. Where must you stay steady? You stay steady in the knowledge that there is no destination, no holy grail, no nirvana, and no alternative ending. You stand up and live. Maybe you take in a movie, maybe you despair, maybe you laugh out loud. You live.

70. This staying steady and this letting go are integral parts of the process of self-authorship. You are a rock and a shape-changer. Looking back, you will recognize yourself and also not recognize yourself at all. How perplexing. And how dynamic!

71. You accept that there will be agitation. You hear yourself thinking something. Is that your own opinion? Or your father's? Or your mother's? Or your rabbi's? Or your culture's? Can you tell? How agitating! You accept that agitation is coming.

72. You accept that there will be a lot of not knowing. Should you choose this path or that one? The law, which has a ring to it, or psychology, which has its own ring, or

animal husbandry? How can you know for sure? Not knowing will not be pleasant!

73. You accept that your instincts are shadowy and powerful. They date from the beginning of time, from pitch-black caves and creatures crawling over you in the dark. You come with strange desires, nightmares, and strangled screams. That is who you are.

74. You accept that the blues may dog your heels. Who is immune to sadness, disappointments, grief, and despair? Your life story will have pages of woe and maybe even chapters. If you could eradicate unhappiness, you would. But how is that possible?

75. You accept that you may find yourself racing out of control. So much is propelling you, chasing you, obsessing you, and making you feverish. You do your best to step to one side, off that speeding conveyor belt, and murmur, "Get a grip, please."

76. You accept that these challenges have come, are here, and are coming. You say, "I may be sad, I may be buffeted, I may be racing, I may be overwhelmed, but I am not losing sight of my twin guiding principles, self-obligation and self-authorship."

77. Will you take breaks from this rigorous work? Of course. You must allow yourself some pancakes, fantastical reveries, lusty side glances, diatribes, catnaps and indulgences. But these are mindful breaks, not serious slips or dangerous meanderings.

78. If, however, you dangerously meander away from self-obligation, if you seriously slip away from self-authorship, if you begin to answer some siren's call, you must leap up,

take that brilliant step to the side, and cry, "Time to right this ship!"

79. Whatever your story has been, however your personality has been baked in, however many times you've slipped and fallen, you locate your freedom and recommit to righteous action. It is like sitting for too long and remembering to stand up again.

80. Steadiness is the string and recommitments are the beads of the necklace. You will not always feel committed. How could you? There are just too many competing ideas and forces. But picture that beautiful necklace with all those recommitments.

81. You coax your best self into existence and employ your best self in the service of your life purposes, your intentions, and your commitments. Then you roll out your movie: part noir mystery, part heartfelt romance, part drama, and part screwball comedy.

82. Will it be a beautiful story? It will be made that much more beautiful by the attention you pay to doing the next right thing. Is a hot shower the next right thing? All right then! Is it that difficult conversation with your daughter? All right then!

83. Will it be a beautiful story? It will be made that much more beautiful by the deep obligation you feel to our noblest sentiments, to those human-sized heroic acts of standing up, speaking out, comforting the afflicted, and sparing the children.

84. Will it be a beautiful story? It will be made that much more beautiful by the care you take in your thinking, in your speaking, and in your actions. Every calm thought, every kind word, every generous act beautifies your story.

85. Will it be a beautiful story? Who can say? But it will be the most honorable and rewarding story you can write. We only rarely see such stories. More usual are stories of self-interest and carelessness. Yours can be ever so much more beautiful than those.

3

BOOK III. INDIVIDUALITY

1. It's likely that you're an individual. Most people are born conventional and prize conformity. But some people prize their individuality. Kirists know to prize theirs. They know that individuality and freedom are linked and even identical.

2. You may have been stubbornly prizing your individuality since birth. That can't have been easy. From the first moments, you were coerced by society to fit in and to look like somebody's idea of normal. You were different; they said, "Be the same!"

3. Even if she trains herself to hold her tongue, an individual will already know as a young child that she can't conform and that she wasn't built to conform. But the pressure applied on her! That pressure is enormous, even back-breaking, even killing.

4. Looking around you, mistrusting the rule-makers, feeling alienated and like a "stranger in a strange land," you find yourself burdened right from the beginning by this

pulsating energy that invites retaliation: the energy of individuality.

5. This fierce need produces lifelong consequences. You find yourself presented with some odd-sounding rule—say, that God will be offended if you don't wear a hat. You find yourself obliged to ask, "Why?" And they will certainly tell you why!

6. The whole world will tell you why. But their answers will not make sense to you. So, you'll get your ears boxed or worse. You'll fall silent or cry, "No, I can't believe this nonsense!" You'll unwillingly acquiesce or grow oppositional.

7. If you take the oppositional route, you'll adamantly reject humbug and try to make personal sense of the world. What will this feel like? Like sorrow, anger, anxiety, alienation, rootlessness, and fierceness, all balled up together.

8. This oppositional attitude, maybe suppressed in childhood, begins to announce itself and assert itself in adolescence and to grow as an individual's interactions with the conventional world increase. A battle begins with all sorts of skirmishes.

9. This oppositional energy grows as his ability to "do his thing" is directly or indirectly restricted by the machinery of society. He finds himself in an odd kind of fight, not necessarily with any particular person or group but with just about everyone.

10. He is in a battle with everything meant to constrain him and reduce him to a cipher. His sees a falsehood there—skirmish! He sees a restriction there— skirmish! He sees

a nonsensical rule there—skirmish! He is marginalized there— skirmish!

11. We repeatedly see this dynamic in the lives of our heroes. Where the dominant ideology challenges reason, they feel obliged to speak out, to do what they believe is right, and to pursue their own goals, even though they may be punished.

12. Popping out of the womb individual, needing to experiment and to risk as part of their individuality, and feeling thwarted and frustrated by the oh-so- conventional universe into which they have been plopped at birth, they wriggle like fish bait.

13. They rush headlong, like a ski jumper down a steep ramp, toward reckless ways of dealing with their feelings of alienation and frustration. Driven to be individual, they race through life, not wisely but fiercely and obsessively.

14. Born individual, you likely have more energy, more charisma, bigger appetites, stronger needs, greater passion, more aliveness, and more avidity than the next person. Individuals often do. Nature saw to this, blindly of course.

15. Nature can't joke or bestow blessings. But this may be nature's way of fueling the individual so that he can be individual. And this extra energy and greater appetite will incline an individual toward addiction, mania and insatiability.

16. How could this supercharging not lead there? How can you have a ton of energy and not court mania? How can you have extra adrenaline and not drive a hundred miles an hour? Nature inadvertently created a fiery, insatiable creature.

17. Nature does not joke but it does produce unintended consequences. One of the major unintended consequences of this extra drive and bigger appetite is that an individual is hard-pressed, and often completely unable, to feel satisfied.

18. You eat a hundred peanuts—not satisfying enough. You write a good book— not satisfying enough. You win the Nobel Prize—not satisfying enough. This inability to get satisfied produces constant background agitation and unhappiness.

19. When nature provides extra energy, it adds susceptibility to mania. When it provides extra ambition, it adds susceptibility to grandiosity. When it provides extra appetite, it adds susceptibility to compulsion. How charming of nature!

20. So, nature, which doesn't joke, nevertheless has its little joke. It creates an individual who must know for himself, follow his own path, and be himself, then heightens his anxiety and makes sure that nothing will satisfy him. Good one, nature!

21. Then there is a second scenario, the scenario of suppressed individuality. This is the more usual path. A person is born individual but succumbs to conformity. Life then feels not quite right or worse. Maybe much, much worse.

22. What does this look like? Here's one version. When I was young I was a thrill-seeker, which led to risky behavior. Things quieted down when I got married and had kids, but that transition was painful and I felt really constricted and limited.

23. We moved to a small farm town where I was

surrounded by religious people who had very strong notions about how you comport yourself, how you raise your kids, what you believe in, and your place in the family and the community.

24. I felt stifled, under-valued and invisible. I wore the mask of a pleasant smile as I served coffee or did the dishes at church functions. I was depressed, I gained a lot of weight, and alcohol became an easy crutch.

25. I've always intuitively mistrusted the status quo but I haven't resisted it enough. I'm a caretaker and people-pleaser and I have a huge desire to fit in and be approved of, all to the detriment of my mental health. I've always cared about survival.

26. Does a third path exist, where a born individual manages to fit beautifully into society? Not on this earth. Either you take the path of individuality and absurd rebellion or you take the demoralizing path of conformity and suppressed individuality.

27. Opt, then, for individuality. You will not fit beautifully into society. You will be begging for skirmishes and battles. Too often you will feel like you are jousting windmills. But this is just another way of saying that you are obliged to do right.

28. Kirists prize their individuality. They also recognize the attendant challenges. There are challenges that come with suppressing their individuality and challenges that come with expressing their individuality. Two very rough roads to travel!

29. We choose the rough road of self-obligation, self-authorship, and self-expression. We need to know for ourselves, do for ourselves, expose humbug, and stand up

to oppressors. We choose the rough road of radical independence.

30. Even if you choose what looks like a conventional goal, say, to be an elementary school teacher, you will still need to pursue that profession as a radically independent individual. Who else but a dedicated individual can stand up for the children?

31. You must stand up because you know that you must. And the results? Much less gorgeous that you might have hoped for. You can't control your principal's temper, the smallness of your curriculum, or the financial straits of your school district.

32. You can't change the fact that your work pays a thousandth of what a fund manager earns. You can't control the fact that your students come in sick and that you get the flu. You can't change the fact that your summer vacation keeps shrinking.

33. And when you stand up as an individual, arguing that religion has crept into the curriculum, that energetic children shouldn't be labeled as disordered, or that a popular teacher is doing too much touching, what's most likely to happen?

34. You'll likely get reprimanded or rebuffed. Sick in bed with the flu, tired of the battles, decades from retirement, and no longer certain that your choice is tenable or makes sense, there you are, living ethically but not at all happy.

35. In a hundred smaller and larger ways, your investment in classroom teaching will likely be threatened. Can you still extract enough satisfaction and coax enough meaning from your choice? That may prove a lifelong challenge.

36. Your hunger for individuality is no blessing. But it is a moral and psychological imperative. You can't both do right and be quiet. You can't both unleash your imagination and conform. Kirists accept that they must be the individual they must be.

37. We make our value-based decisions and then we try to live up to them and live with them, simultaneously feeling proud and blue. We're careful not to inadvertently call this state of sadness, agitation and insufficient satisfaction "depression."

38. Our malaise is no "mental disorder" but rather the natural consequence of dropping a passionate, energetic, creative, moral, and lively creature into this tiny little world, a world full of roadblocks, tyrants, disappointments and ordinariness.

39. So, the results we get do not match our hopes. Ideally, we would get excellent results from choosing righteous work like teaching and tackling that work as an engaged individual. Ideally, we would find ourselves smiling a lot and even happy.

40. In reality, we're likely to get very mixed results and do a lot of frowning. This is why the life a kirist leads will not look like arithmetic. When we do math, we get a satisfying answer like "Four." When we do life, our answers look very different.

41. Instead of four, we get: "I intend to write my poetry, even though it will never pay, live in love, even though I'm only mediocre relationship material, and raise children in love, even though I'm terribly scared of my critical nature."

42. Or: "I see that I'm responsible for the whole world,

which is ridiculous, and that I must call out every injustice, which is a fool's errand, and that I'm obliged to do great work, even though my first efforts have been completely awful."

43. Or: "I need to live in this community, because my loved ones reside here and won't leave, but this community is tyrannical, dogmatic, and anti-rational. So, I'll stay here but resist, even though that is bound to threaten me and my loved ones."

44. None of this sounds like fun. Nor is it. Individuality is not a cheerful game or a stroll through the park. It is a tight-fitting suit that nature has fitted you with, making every step of the way half-uncomfortable. No need to thank nature for this!

45. This mandate to individuality is a lifelong albatross. Nature fitted you with this albatross and now you ratify its presence on your shoulder. You say, "I didn't ask for this pressure but I accept it, since I refuse to live small or to shut my eyes."

46. Can we meet these challenges? Not at the 90% level. Not at the 80% level. The challenges presented by our fierce need to be individual reduce us to accepting a very modest success rate, above insignificant but well below satisfactory.

47. Your individuality demands that you write an excellent novel. It is great in spots and ordinary in spots and terrible in spots. Was that an insignificant effort? No. Do you feel satisfied? No. Challenge bravely tackled, leading to a 20% victory.

48. Your individuality demands that you denounce the immoral practices in your profession. Your peers mock you

and make sure that you get no business. But the outside world listens a little. Challenge bravely tackled, leading to a 9% victory.

49. Your individuality demands that you see for yourself what's beyond the horizon. This leads to some excellent adventures and some terrible misadventures. You come home wiser and battered. Challenge bravely tackled, leading to a 12% victory.

50. Even if we do manage to persevere—to write our poems, to battle our windmills, to right some wrongs—it is not without a thousand ups and downs, countless frustrations and disappointments, and every manner of rage and dirge.

51. A kirist accepts this reality, learns from experience, and creates her marching orders. She may spend her days in a kitchen or an office but that doesn't mean that she isn't marching. She is continuously choosing to be her authentic self.

52. Individuality demands choosing. Maybe you wonder if you ought to continue at your current job. Maybe you wonder if you should embark on a screenplay. Maybe you wonder if you should point out a wrong. How will you choose?

53. Not by attending a workshop. Not by visiting an astrologer. Not by seeking out a pastor. Not by reading a self-help book. Not by calling a psychic. Not by consulting a psychiatrist. You take that kirist step to one side, face the matter, and decide.

54. You look to your own answers. Maybe you are not in a position to diagnose your prickly rash or to know if you've written an effective contract. Maybe those are questions

for experts. But for life questions, you are your own expert.

55. You decide which are the worthy actions and which are the unworthy actions. You decide what to value and how to make sense of your many often-contradictory values, values that awkwardly tumble together in real-life situations.

56. And you remember to serve the good. Kirists serve the good. You do not take your mandate to individuality as license to grandiosity, narcissism or naked self- interest. This isn't so easy to accomplish, as all that greed wants to keep bubbling up.

57. Isn't the pull to individuality going to incline you toward a demanding personality where you feel entitled to interrupt, out-shout, ignore, trample, dismiss, sulk and strive arrogantly for what you want? Kirists know this narcissism is in them.

58. The more you proudly invoke your individuality, the more you may find yourself in conflict between kirist modesty and native grandiosity, between kirist goodness and genetic self-interest, between kirist individuality and simple narcissism.

59. To handle this conflict may require that you encourage a personality upgrade. Who would you like to be ideally? A kirist asks that bold question and invites up an answer. Are you already your best you? That's highly unlikely.

60. Maybe you repeatedly behave in a cruel way, because you were humiliated as a child and find it viscerally satisfying to destroy others. As the universe does not arbitrate meaning, you have that option available to you. But a kirist refuses.

61. Maybe you like to storm about because you thrive on drama. Maybe you've gotten into the habit of blaming and hating. Maybe you've left the battlefield and gone into hiding. You've ended up somewhere—but that mustn't be the end point.

62. Maybe out of anxiety you leave things undone and avoid living your life purposes. The universe has no way to reduce your anxiety and, by virtue of its starkness and relentlessness, only increases it. Kirists must create their own calmness.

63. Maybe your edge isn't grandiosity or arrogance but meekness and passivity. Then your personality upgrade would look very different from a narcissist's. Yours might look like a fierce warrior butterfly finally emerging from its cocoon of safety.

64. Just as we accept the burdens of individuality, self-obligation, self-authorship, absurd rebellion, and goodness, we accept the burden of transforming ourselves into a more ideal version of ourselves, into the kirist version of ourselves.

65. We use our freedom to step to one side, to gaze into the full-length mirror hanging there, and to make conscious decisions about who we intend to be. We come into the world already somebody, our personality forms, and then we upgrade it.

66. This is the kirist journey from personality to personhood. You look at life and you look at yourself and you say, "To honor my individuality and to meet my obligations to myself, I must transform myself into someone much better equipped."

67. But even then, you will only be better equipped, not

perfectly equipped. You'll improve your navigation skills as you author your story but you can't guarantee sailing to the right country or avoiding a shipwreck when you try to land there.

68. Where will your individuality take you? To some highly uncomfortable places. Maybe you'll embark on some quest you can't explain or name. There you are, wandering about, announcing that you are on a quest but getting nowhere.

69. Maybe you'll find yourself pondering the biggest questions and refusing to accept too-simple answers, only to discover that the biggest questions have no satisfactory answers. You were hungry for resolution but all you got was confusion.

70. Maybe your mandate to do some good got all mixed up with your desire to make a splash and live well. Now you find yourself in a comfortable position in a corner office, doing much less good than you know that you ought to be doing.

71. That is, challenges will remain. You can feel smug when you do math, since two plus two will equal four forever. But life does not permit you to feel smug about it. We face that and say, "A lone individual has always mattered and always will."

72. A lone individual can stand up to a row of tanks, with the whole world watching. The tanks will win but that image of freedom will be seared into the brains of children and may prove pivotal fifty years later, as other tanks are gathering.

73. A lone individual, sitting on a city council, can prove the tie-breaking vote that keeps the thieves from further

thievery or the polluters from making further misery. Or she can sit on a higher bench and save democracy.

74. A lone individual can tell a quiet story, maybe about a rabbit disappearing down a rabbit hole and the little girl who follows him into Wonderland, that is read by a lot of children, or maybe just a few, and that encourages their individuality.

75. A lone individual can find a cure, help a child in need, or start a rights' movement. She may need to be a medical researcher in order to find that cure but she can be a complete amateur and still aid that child or launch that movement.

76. Lone individuals can also work together. Each, being an individual, may well prove testy, opinionated and difficult. But testy, opinionated and difficult individuals, as long as they are not inflexible, can change hearts and move mountains.

77. Gatherings of individuals, as for instance at a Continental Congress, can prove momentous. Each will have his or her own agenda, but if they happen to be a gathering of kirists you might get a wall torn down or new rights for everyone.

78. The world is better off in each of these instances. It is not changed; it is not transformed; it is not saved. But it is better off than if that lone individual had not existed. That "better off" is the epitome of kirist modesty and kirist excellence.

79. The world is better off in each of these instances and kirists know it. They might wish that a lone individual could do more and they might wish that they themselves

could do more. But they do not characterize what they can do as nothing.

80. On a given day, you may find yourself with no particular chance to assert your individuality and no particular reason to assert your individuality. There may be many quiet days of sharing, joining, fitting in, helping and accommodating.

81. But on another day, maybe even the very next day, you may be called on. On that day, you shake your head a little and murmur, "Here we go again." Self-obligation and self-authorship demand that murmur and the action that follows.

82. Fighting to retain your individuality may have made you cranky and morose. As a new kirist, feel reinvigorated. You have been reminded that individuality is not fruitless, quixotic stubbornness but rather exactly what is required of you.

83. Suppressing your individuality may have made you ill and despairing. As a new kirist, open the window, lean out, and say a little something. You don't have to shout, not at first. Just hum a tune of freedom and feel the sun on your face.

84. It would be lovely if our efforts produced the results we craved. But life is not a romance. We opt for value, not rewards, we stand up, we assert our individuality, and we serve the good. If we're also rewarded, we smile wryly.

85. Be the individual that you are. You could certainly choose safety instead; and on some days, you likely ought to choose safety. But on those many other days, venturing out alone, say what needs saying and do what needs doing.

4

BOOK IV. ABSURD REBELLION

1. A kirist is easier with absurdity than the next person. We accept the reality of absurdity, we do not deny its demoralizing power, and we wish that life was less absurd than it is. But above all, we exclaim, "I refuse to let absurdity rob me of the freedom I possess."

2. There was a time, for the better part of a hundred and fifty years, when public and private conversations about absurdity flourished in a corner of human discourse. Everyday people were not discussing it but we were, you and I, usually privately.

3. Mostly privately, we looked at life, shook our heads, and said, "How absurd!" How absurd that we should be given consciousness of our own mortality and made to feel terrible. How absurd that we should be born doomed—and know it!

4. How absurd that the details of your birth should matter so much. How absurd that you might come into the world

burdened by ordinary looks, tyrants for parents, stubby legs, and a dismal outlook. Who threw those miserable dice?

5. How absurd that virtue was not rewarded. How absurd that the self-proclaimed righteous were so devious and untruthful. How absurd that the rich got richer and the poor poorer. How absurd that there should be upper classes and lower classes.

6. So much looked absurd that whole movements grew up whose sole agenda was to point out the absurdity of this or that: the absurdity of employing a word like "truth," the absurdity of valuing art, the absurdity of political action, and so on.

7. Then we stopped thinking about absurdity, talking about absurdity, or factoring it into our calculations about life. We simply concluded that life was a cheat, included absurdity in that evaluation, and dropped the concept like a hot potato.

8. We arrived at a point where it seemed absurd to continue chatting about absurdity. We still took absurdity as a bedrock feature of existence but it became a secret, unmentionable feature. We buried it and we sank further into despair.

9. We turned our back on the concept and tried to put it out of our mind, even as life grew more absurd. We swallowed hard, ran this way and that, kept very busy, and purchased antidepressants. But who were we fooling or kidding?

10. We had made a serious mistake, a grave miscalculation, by trying to turn our back on absurdity. Now it is time to

face it again. Let us exclaim "How absurd!" as we look out at the human spectacle. Yes, that hurts, but we are obliged to be honest.

11. And it does hurt. It hurts because we know that it translates as, "Life is ridiculous," "life isn't fair," "nothing really matters," and so on. We may exclaim "How absurd!" with a bit of a laugh, as if we've amused ourselves, but that laugh is deeply bitter.

12. Now we must revisit those absurdities, as bitter as they make us feel, for the sake of understanding our real challenges and crafting our next steps. Here are a few of those absurdities, just a sampling, about as many as we need or can stomach.

13. I may be a person who values helping the less fortunate and I may also be a cynical person who wonders if the panhandler I'm passing is perhaps a professional beggar playing me. How absurd that I am both people! But I am.

14. I am the same person in the morning and in the afternoon. I possess the same values. But how those values play themselves out—what predominates, what comes forward, what "wins"—is so very different those few hours apart. How absurd!

15. You read an interview and are once again shocked to discover the extent to which powerful forces in society are mugging you and gagging you. You really should fight back, shouldn't you? But how absurd to imagine fighting back! Fight back? Really?

16. Having read that demoralizing interview, you know in your heart that you should drop everything and fight. But isn't that completely absurd? What difference could you

possibly make? And there you sit, precisely as impotent as you feel.

17. But isn't it likewise completely absurd to simply go about your business as if you hadn't noticed? Here you are, working fifty hours a week at a terrible job so that you can pay the rent in an overpriced city, and they steal from you. And you do nothing?

18. And not only can't you fight back, maybe you don't really want to fight. Maybe all you want to do is write your psychological thriller set in 1920's Paris. But what is the value in that? Who needs another story? How absurd to devote your life to that!

19. And maybe you value your loved one above all else? But what if he is about to engage in some terrible betrayal or some sordid deed? Should you still side with him, this love of your life, perhaps to your everlasting shame? How absurd!

20. Or, say, you completely understand mass entertainment. All of that sedating, soothing, and sentimentalizing so as to seduce mesmerized viewers into forgetfulness. But your five-year-old really wants to see a certain Disney movie. How absurd!

21. Should you deny him that innocent pleasure? Should you have a conversation with him in which you quote Adorno that "Walt Disney is the most dangerous man in America"? Or do you let him watch that singing mermaid? What an absurd situation!

22. And, more absurd still, maybe you are an animator who would love to work on such movies! You see through them, you despise them, and you also love them and want

to be a part of creating them. Really, could anything be more absurd?

23. If we had the stomach for it, we could continue with countless examples. Instead, let's distill the essence: absurdity is with us, even as we try to deny it. And it is better to face it, whether bitterly or with ringing laughter, and then get on with living.

24. Yes, it may be absurd to bother. But the absurdity of bothering must not be allowed to stand as the perfect excuse for inaction. We nod at absurdity, we give it its due, and then we act. You acknowledge absurdity without letting absurdity defeat you.

25. Absurdity is not an excuse for inaction. It certainly could be. Can you think of a more powerful excuse for not bothering than the absurdity of bothering? But as someone who has decided to matter, you refuse to take that familiar, well-lighted route.

26. In Camus's famous fable, Sisyphus, condemned by the gods to roll his rock up a mountain for all eternity, smiles at the absurdity of his situation. But in his peculiar way he has it easy. He can't act freely, which means that he is nothing like you.

27. Sisyphus has no options and no way to matter. Oppressed and rendered completely impotent, he smiles the dignified, mostly vacant smile of a man no longer with us, a living dead man, one who for all intents and purposes is smiling from the afterlife.

28. Sisyphus can take no action in the real world. He can respond with dignity and with his peculiar smile to his situation but his situation is not yours. He is trapped in a sense

even more monumental than yours. You can still do some good!

29. You are not Sisyphus. You are a man with a toothache and options, a woman with heartaches and choices. Your delicate amount of freedom, pitted against that ocean of absurdity, is your absurd burden to bear and your responsibility to manifest.

30. You, having smiled wryly at the absurdity of it all, must go about your impossible business. You acknowledge that it is absurd to stand alone, tired, out of sorts, and only wanting brunch, but there you are, rising to your feet and standing.

31. Sisyphus is wearing an ironic smile. Your smile is graver. You have your small portion of freedom, that portion that you are obliged to use, which makes it much harder for you to smile at all. Maybe you find that you can't smile. But still you can act.

32. It is ridiculous that a purposeless universe should make it so hard on us, effectively acting, in its completely indifferent way, as if it were actually malevolent. Ridiculous ... but here we are. So, we do not bow. Rather, we rebel. Our absurd rebellion!

33. We know that absurd rebellion is the right way. When we encounter a character in literature who ought to rebel and doesn't, we want to shake him. Sir, can't you see the absurdity of your situation and that your only wise response is rebellion?

34. In Kafka's The Trial, K. hunts for rational answers to his absurd situation. Finally, he is absurdly executed. Watching him, we want to scream, "Stop it already! Don't

you see that rebellion is your only answer! A ridiculous answer; but still your only one!"

35. We want K. to refuse to sheepishly play along. We want him to laugh just once at the absurdity of his situation, so as to unlock the door to some resistance. Please, K., laugh at the absurdity of your indictment and your punishment. And rebel!

36. Of course, some rebellions are impossible. You can't stop the sun from slowly dying. You can't stop time from passing. You can't stop falls from hurting. You can't stop your mind from whirring. You might as well beg electricity to stop shocking.

37. And then there are all those pointless rebellions. Spending the week fighting that unfair service charge on your bill. Refusing a seat on the bus because you hate looking old. And so many other rebellions that waste your time and do not serve you.

38. Skip the pointless rebellions and the impossible rebellions. Skip those rebellions that arise just because you're angry or hurt. Skip those rebellions that are just versions of acting out. Skip those rebellions that do not serve you or the world.

39. Which rebellions, then, are the absurd rebellions that are the hallmark and cornerstone of kirism? They are your absurd rebellions on the side of the good. They are your rebellions for the benefit of all humankind, played out in tiny installments.

40. You might rebel by singing. It's absurd to suppose that your protest song can stop the tidal wave of history. But you sing it anyway. You sing it on street corners and from

rooftops. You sing out for justice, a rebel songbird, not caring if you look ridiculous.

41. You might rebel by breaking the silence. Can your few kind words, offered in passing, do much good? You sigh, put aside your distaste for your species, and stop and chat anyway. You say a nice thing to this person who needs some comforting.

42. You might rebel by putting the world on your shoulders. It's absurd to suppose that it's your job to save the world. What could be more ridiculous? And still anything less is too little. Everyone tells you, "Do less," and you say, "No, I don't think so."

43. You might rebel against your own programming. How absurd to arm-wrestle yourself! But you know about your shadow side, your trickster nature, your callous impulses, your venalities, and, absurdly enough, you valiantly rebel against your own nature.

44. You might rebel against the very idea that you do not matter. Yes, you are puny. Yes, you are a lone creature among billions and billions of others. Yes, you are miniscule. But do not let your insignificance stop you from aiming for grandeur.

45. What are you rebelling against? The universe deeming you trivial. Yes, it has done that to you. But you say, "I am something, in my human way, and when it comes to speaking up, pointing a finger, and of all that, I will make my presence known."

46. What are you rebelling against? The hypnotic trance that afflicts all of us, causing us to sit there, watching yet another episode of a beautifully crafted television show

about nothing. We rebel by snapping our fingers and waking up.

47. What are you rebelling against? The mountains of humbug piled in every corner of the kingdom, where deodorant is sold to make poverty smell good and holes in the ozone layer are called windows on the universe. We rebel against liars.

48. What are you rebelling against? You rebel against the inertia produced by living, the inertia that makes sitting on the couch seem like your next best option. You heroically create your own momentum to fight the terrible weight of inertia.

49. What are you rebelling against? You rebel against meanness, even if you are feeling mean yourself, because you know that meanness wounds and that you are not here to do harm or let others do harm. You take a stand against meanness.

50. What are you rebelling against? You rebel against your own modesty and your own meekness, qualities drilled into you by your family and your society. You roar like a lion even if you have been trained to squeak like a mouse.

51. What are you rebelling against? You rebel against your own disinclination to rebel. How comical that you are in mortal combat with yourself about rebelling! Imagine a squirrel fighting with itself about whether or not to crack open a nut.

52. Squirrels are not built that way. No squirrel can find itself in so absurd a situation as we find ourselves. We find ourselves built with the good sense to avoid conflict and the good sense to invite conflict for the sake of righteousness. How trying!

53. How are you rebelling? By speaking up rather than keeping silent. Your vocal chords are instruments of goodness. You are that child who says, in a small voice but one so distinct that everyone can hear him, "Look, the Emperor has no clothes!"

54. How are you rebelling? By navigating your personal way through the mine fields of custom and ordinariness, building what you need as you go, creating the tools, the methods, the systems, the visions, the world of you.

55. How are you rebelling? By announcing, "I will not buy religions and philosophies that do not speak to me and that do not make sense to me. That a billion people believe something signifies nothing. Not a billion or a trillion. It has to make sense to me!"

56. And then there are all the quiet rebellions. You want to party. Nothing in the universe can stop you. There is no one to keep you from your drugs, your sex, your fun. Why not party? Still, you sigh and stay home. Absurd rebellion looks like this.

57. Everyone is saying that your son should be medicated for his high spirits. They are cocksure and certain. You disagree. You say, maybe in a shout or maybe very quietly, "No, thanks. I'm not buying what you're selling." Your rebellion spares him.

58. You tiptoe to the mirror and carefully look. "Oh," you say, "I think I need to upgrade myself here. Oh, and also there. I must calm myself. And lose that weight. And shed that guilt. And smile more. And roar more. And feel more devoted. I see!"

59. You quietly make those changes, some earthshaking, some painstaking, some as bite-sized as getting on your walking

shoes and walking to work, even though you could manage fifteen or twenty more minutes of work time if you didn't.

60. Surely it is absurd to walk to work when there is so much to do there and you are so far behind. Nevertheless, you calmly rebel against the pull to rush like a maniac. You stroll to work, feeling the sun on your face, falling behind but also getting ahead.

61. Most crucially, you quietly rebel in the service of the good. That is your understanding of how you want to live your life: on the side of the good. You acknowledge the absurd difficulty and amazing complexity of right action and nevertheless vote for it.

62. You quietly rebel in the service of what ought to be. You look at what is and say, "It ought to be thus." You muse on betterment and listen to your soft musings. Maybe you move the species forward or maybe you just proceed like an inchworm.

63. You quietly rebel in the direction of an improved, upgraded you. You look in the mirror and you say, "I could be better, and here's how." Softly, softly, walking on tiptoes, you discard a vice, act with love, refuse to shout, or calm your nerves a little.

64. Is it absurd to lead when following is so much safer and more convenient? Absurd to discard a beloved vice when it's doing no particular harm? Absurd to do good when the universe is completely indifferent? No; these rebellions are the best of us.

65. These absurd rebellions are available to everyone. They are not available only to the privileged, the healthy, the educated, or the nicely positioned. Each human being

can live an engaged life, even in the direst of circumstances, if he or she is willing.

66. Well, but what can absurd rebellion look like to an old woman in a wheelchair parked in a nursing home corridor? Or to a refugee carrying his belongings on his back? Or to a gay teenager trapped in a claustrophobic town? What then?

67.What does absurd rebellion look like to each of them? For the old woman, it might mean taking three painful steps with a walker. The refugee might become a camp leader. The gay youth might plot his escape. These are things they might try.

68. Each can do something and each must do something. There is no formulaic response to suggest and no principle to offer, except the principle of radical self- authorship: a human being can stand up, even if he or she can't literally stand up.

69. No one is in a perfect position to rebel. It would be absurd to imagine that there could be some perfect position. We are all too burdened, too constrained, too conflicted, too human. We awkwardly stand on one foot and rebel while tilting.

70. And, of course, there will be consequences. You tell the truth at work—job gone. You back an unpopular cause—serious pushback. Are you ready for such consequences? Of course not. How absurd to imagine you could be ready for harsh reality!

71. You see those consequences looming and you hear yourself say, "No, thank you. No absurd rebellion for me. The price is just too high." Then you are obliged to shake

your head and reply, "But isn't the price of not rebelling even higher?"

72. The price of not rebelling when rebelling is called for is despair. That despair is crippling millions. They may have no idea how to name their malaise and they may have no idea that absurd rebellion is called for, consequences be damned. But it is.

73. Are you ready? No. No creature of our sort can ever really be ready. So, unsure, weak in the knees, you nod and say, "I am not ready. But that's just another bit of absurdity, to suppose that a creature like me could ever be ready for such heroism!"

74. Absurd rebellion is you taking your stand even though you feel alone. You don your winter coat to help with the coldness and you warm your hands by the fire, where other hands are also warming. You stay as warm as you can in the face of cosmic coldness.

75. Why engage in absurd rebellion when others aren't? Because you must. Let others fall short, even pathetically short, of self-authorship and self-obligation. Your path is the harder one but the righteous one. Don't you feel that?

76. Others may resent you for living more heroically than they are. That is absurd, too, that your neighbors might resent you for standing up. And maybe we should even envy them, as they look to be absurdity-proof! But, no, nothing to envy there.

77. Still, we must remain watchful. The kirist way is courageous and dangerous. We may nod compassionately at this odd creature that nature has made and then dropped into a hornet's nest. But as much compassion as we may feel, we must be careful.

78. It is absurd that we must be reckless in our rebellions and also careful in our rebellions! It is reckless of us to rebel, as there will be consequences, and so we take as much care as we can. But in the end, we do what we must, as that is our obligation.

79. You see a child smile. That smile changes nothing and that smile changes everything. You are built to be moved by that smile and it reminds you of your obligations. Maybe you smile, too; but whether you smile or not, you have your work to do.

80. What if everyone in one tumultuous gasp exclaimed, "How absurd! Now let me get on with it!" That would amount to a leap forward for our species. We would all of a sudden grow up. That leap is not coming—except person by person.

81. What a triumphant sound such a mass exhalation would make! It would help every person in every situation. It would help our species and our world. But there will never be a mass exhalation. It will always be just a single person sighing.

82. Denying the absurd is a powerful obstacle to living your life purposes, manifesting your potential, and coaxing meaning into existence. Instead of denying it, you acknowledge absurdity and calculate your rebellions.

83. Our tasks are absurd, our efforts are absurd, and our situation is absurd. Yes, there will be infant deaths, cancers, fascists, meaningless work, hurricanes, split second mistakes that result in AIDS. We can't bear this … but we can respond to this.

84. We marshal our freedom, shake our head, and say, "This is absurd and maybe even intolerable but here I go

anyway." Then we find a hand to hold, a mouth to kiss, or a battle to wage. That is what wellness looks like.

85. We possess a bit of freedom and the absurd obligation, arising from nowhere but our own understanding of our situation, to use it. We are obliged because we understand that we are obliged. Hello, absurd rebel. Nice to see you again.

5

BOOK V. THE LOGIC OF LIFE PURPOSES

1. No one can explain consciousness, not what it is or why we have it. But here we are. We are conscious and that defines us. From consciousness flows everything: our thinking, our imagining, our comprehending, our deciding, and so on.

2. Consciousness produces everything that we are, which is much more than just a creature with senses and some limited awareness. We are not just aware, as in, "Oh, there's a butterfly!" We are astute, as in, "Oh, that is a rare butterfly!"

3. Consciousness produces the mind and the experience of in-dwelling, that subjective experience of "being somewhere inside." That is where we muse, pester ourselves, daydream, write poetry, and feel sad about the state of the world.

4. One of the things that we do as we in-dwell is wonder about our importance or unimportance, cosmically, to others, and to ourselves. Likewise, we wonder about the

importance or unimportance of the things that we are doing or intend to do.

5. Bound up with these conversations are two culture-driven ideas: "the meaning of life" and "the purpose of life." Kirists understand that these two phrases are powerful traps that have confused and tormented humans for the longest time.

6. These two phrases have come to be for a variety of reasons, some having to do with how language works, some with our desire not to feel unimportant, some with the needs of authoritarian institutions to sustain and promote themselves.

7. First, the very shape of those phrases makes it seem as if there is or must be some singular meaning to life and some singular purpose to life. By creating those phrases, we create the idea, and with the idea all sorts of unnecessary longings.

8. Without language creating those ideas, along with what for many people is lifelong confusion, you might just peel a potato, fight for justice, hold your child's hand, and get on with life. You would find life itself real and already important.

9. Second, those phrases have built into them the idea of a universe run by someone or something that has created a grand pageant where we get to play our part, as if we'd won a leading role in a play. If, that is, we only knew our part.

10. Third, our religious, spiritual, political and other authoritarian leaders promote these phrases, because these phrases set you up to believe that there is exactly "one true

thing" in life, say the demand to serve God, to defend your race, and so on.

11. People have long been seduced, transfixed and pestered by these phrases and that has led to a very large, very negative outcome. When they can't envision or discern "the purpose of life" or "the meaning of life," they feel bereft and lost.

12. Life got much darker because people have been hunting for something that doesn't exist. If you suppose that there is "a purpose to life" and "a meaning to life" and you can't figure out what they are, how are you going to feel? Miserable.

13. You're going to feel confused, upset at yourself for what looks to be your failure at discernment, and maybe angry at the universe for playing what looks to be a sadistic game. You are not going to feel at all well, emotionally or existentially.

14. Part of the power of this trap is that it feels frightening to think the reverse, that "there is no meaning to life" or "there is no purpose to life." To billions, these rejections of millennia of dogma sound too terrible to countenance.

15. Kirists reject those false phrases and also the false negative constructions of those phrases. Both "there is a meaning to life" and "there is no meaning to life" are wrong-headed responses to reality. Exactly the same with "purpose."

16. Those twin phrases, "the meaning of life" and "the purpose of life," have never pointed to anything real or true. Rather, they are constructed concoctions. They function to confuse and to disempower and kirists deconstruct and reject them.

17. Kirists say a different thing instead. First, they say, "There is no singular purpose to life. Rather there are our individual life purpose choices. I decide what is important enough for me to organize my life around and then I live exactly that life."

18. With regard to meaning, kirists say, "Of course, there is something that ought to be called 'meaning.' It is a certain sort of psychological experience and a certain sort of idea. Human beings really do have those experiences and those ideas."

19. Kirists add, "There are an abundant number of psychological experiences of meaning. Yes, the sensation of meaning does come and go, like any other feeling. But that doesn't make meaning unreal. It just makes it quixotic and transitory."

20. Meaning doesn't come down from on high. It is just another artifact of human consciousness. We are built to think about meaning, to love its presence and to be upset by its absence, and to sometimes (and only sometimes) experience it.

21. Therefore, meaning is a wellspring. There is always the possibility that in the next moment we may experience it. We can train ourselves to coax it into existence, to not miss it so much when it is absent, and to understand its place in life.

22. Meaning isn't as important as we've talked ourselves into believing it is. It is 'just' a certain sort of psychological experience. A good and worthy life can go on (and must go on) even if we aren't having enough of those experiences.

23. If I am doing the next right thing, then that is the next right thing to be doing, whether or not it happens to

feel meaningful. If it feels meaningful, that is wonderful. If it doesn't, we maturely just get on living our life purposes.

24. When a kirist says, "Nothing is inherently meaningful," doesn't that seem to fly in the face of reality? Aren't some things just clearly "meaningful," like, say, walking in nature, looking at gorgeous art, or spending time with the grandkids?

25. No. Nothing is universally meaningful by virtue of it feeling meaningful to lots of people lots of the time. Maybe you experience meaning playing with your grand-kids. Or maybe you experience boredom and the desire to be elsewhere.

26. There is nothing "intrinsically meaningful" about playing with the grandkids, walking in nature, looking at art, or anything else. Yes, these may provoke the experi-ence of meaning, as we are built to experience them as meaningful. But that's all.

27. There is a huge difference between the idea that certain aspects of existence are intrinsically meaningful versus the idea that something may sometimes (or even often) provoke the experience of meaning. All the differ-ence in the world!

28. The first is a fiction and a trap. The second is the exact truth. Consciousness craves meaning and human beings are in the position to make meaning investments, to seize meaning opportunities, and to try to coax the experience they crave.

29. We crave meaning and, if we are lucky, we can coax it into existence. Likewise, we crave a sense of purpose; and here our task is to identify what we deem important and to

choose exactly those as our purposes. We make life purpose choices.

30. How will you make your life purpose choices? How will you decide which are the activities and the states of being you deem most important to you? Well, first of all, they must be important to you. You arbitrate your life purposes.

31. Your culture may say, "Turn over your life to taking care of your aging parents." You get to decide if you agree. Your government may say, "Fight in this all-important war." You get to decide if you agree. You may; or you may not.

32. Similarly, you may be told that this is not something you ought to concern yourself with or that this is something that you really must not do. Do not be gay. Do not be altruistic. Do not be a whistleblower. You get to decide if you agree.

33. Whatever is maximized or minimized by others, validated or stigmatized by others, all of that is for you to step aside from, taking that vital kirist step to the side, that crucial sidestep to awareness, and to ponder, consider, and decide about.

34. You are necessarily deciding only for now, making provisional, full-throated, whole-hearted commitments. It must only be for now, as you do not know how life will play itself out. At the same time, these must be full-throated commitments.

35. And what if nothing seems important enough to elevate to the "high place" of life purpose choice? Well, that probably means that you're in crisis and maybe have been in crisis for a long time. It's hard to live when nothing feels very important.

36. If you find yourself in that unfortunate position, you must start doing some anointing. This sounds like, "My novel, the world, love, nothing feels very important. But I am going to make the decision to consider them important. I'd better!"

37. To summarize: we make our life purpose choices and then we live them. We stop making a fuss about meaning and at the same time we try to coax the experience of meaning into existence. We live our life purposes and we coax meaning.

38. We shift from pestering ourselves about "the purpose of life" and we make our idiosyncratic life purpose choices. Maybe we encapsulate those purposes in a single phrase, like "I do the next right thing," or maybe we create a list or a menu.

39. You may never have done this work before. You may have insights into your nature, an excellent sense of your strengths and weaknesses, possess strong feelings about how the world operates, but have never previously done this precise work.

40. Kirists do this work. They ask themselves, "What should my life purposes be?" or "What do I consider really important?" They know that any answer they arrive at must be provisional but that doesn't stop them from making those vital decisions.

41. You may find yourself reluctant to make this effort. Why? Because by naming your life purposes, you set the bar very high. If, say, you assert that your primary life purpose is to do the next right thing, then you have to do the next right thing.

42. And you must keep at it, next right thing after next

right thing, forever. How much work you just made for yourself! Isn't it easier to keep "seeking" meaning and purpose, even though there is nothing to find? But kirists know better.

43. If you say that one of your life purposes is to write fiction in your most passionate and powerful voice, well, you have to sit there, day in and day out, on the many bad days as well as on the good ones, and struggle to write that powerful fiction.

44. If you announce that you want to love and be loved, you have to actually love and you actually have to be loveable. This may necessitate a huge personality upgrade and some real movement away from grandiosity, arrogance, and narcissism.

45. These are not easy things. Making life purpose choices sets us up for real work. You decide to be a parent—and then you have kids. You decide to be an activist—and you put your body on the line. No wonder that we may be reluctant!

46. We may also feel undermined by some core doubt, a doubt that sounds like the following: "Coming up with my life purposes feels so artificial and so arbitrary. Maybe life really wants something completely different from me!"

47. Or it may sound like the following: "What I want and what I believe in seems to shift all the time. Maybe there really isn't any such thing as life purposes? Maybe there are only whims, desires, cravings, and nothing more substantial than air!"

48. Or it may sound like: "Human beings are such disposable, self-centered, trivial creatures—what a lot of silly

arrogance to talk about life purposes when most people seem closer to the insect world!"

49. Or it may sound like: "I am such a slave to my appetites—what a joke to think about life purposes! I can hardly stop myself from eating peanuts or shopping online day and night. Life purposes! I'm nothing but a walking addiction!"

50. These doubts take on countless forms. And our inclination to doubt isn't helped by the fact that the people who promote the idea of a singular life purpose present the picture that "the purpose of life" must be sought out and chased after.

51. Naturally you may doubt that you know your life purposes if everyone is telling you that they are out there somewhere and that you need to keep seeking them. Find, find, find—that is the life purpose mantra. Life as an Easter egg hunt!

52. Kirists learn to navigate their way through this language maze and to stand firm in their determination not to seek what doesn't exist but instead to name their life purposes and to live their life purposes. They opt for living over seeking.

53. You might name your life purposes in a list sort of way: for example, "I want to create, be of service, be an activist in support of certain causes, cultivate strong, meaningful relationships, and live calmly and also passionately."

54. What might your list look like? Maybe: to make use of your talents, to have some successes, to love and be loved, to feel alive and connected, to not fail yourself, to do the right thing, to stay healthy, and a few more. Something like that?

55. Your list might be shorter, longer, or completely different from the above. Yours might include concrete items, like "Spend five hours a day on my home business." Or it might include beautiful, fanciful, lofty items like, "Save the world."

56. How many life purposes do you require? Is there some ideal or magic number, like five or seven or nine? Can there be too many? Can there be too few? Probably "yes" is the answer to the last two: there likely can be too many and also too few!

57. For instance, will it work to have just a single life purpose? Fighting injustice or being of service are lovely life purpose choices. But would it work to hold one of those as the only thing you deem important? Can a life be organized that way?

58. Kirists come to doubt that organizing a life around just one life purpose, even one as profound as battling injustice or being of service, will quite work. In reality, we deem many things important, not just this one thing or that one thing.

59. A solid kirist life seems to require something more like: "I will make use of my talents every single day in the service of truth-telling and my other important values, while getting satisfaction out of life through love and righteous work."

60. You might also condense your several life purpose choices into a simple phrase, for instance "I do the next right thing." Kirists discover that having both, both a menu of life purposes and a life purpose statement, is an excellent idea.

61. And so, doing this work and living this way, the anxiety

of seeking and not finding may end. The despair of living without purpose may end. Panic around meaninglessness may end. Your battle to feel motivated may resolve itself.

62. We identify our life purposes, we commit to living them, we see this identifying and this committing as centerpiece activities of self-obligation, self-authorship, and absurd rebellion. We do this … and then all sorts of shifts occur.

63. Our life purposes can and will shift. Maybe parenting is not important to us in our twenties and very important to us in our thirties. Maybe foreign travel is very important to us in our thirties and not important to us in our eighties.

64. Because of these shifts, we can come to the wrong conclusion that we have only transitory desires, not anything like life purposes. But a change in particulars doesn't mean that our life purpose choices weren't real at the time we made them.

65. The compact car you owned was real. So was the minivan you needed when the kids came. The minivan didn't make a lie out of the compact. You didn't "not know your own mind." Life changed and with it came new life purpose decisions.

66. You might try something, because it feels interesting and right. Maybe it's a certain graduate program. Three weeks in, you sense that it is much less interesting and right than you hoped it would be. Of course, this is a dreadful experience.

67. But does that outcome imply that you hadn't made a strong life purpose choice? No. It only means that you made an investment in something that appears not to be

paying dividends. You bit into something and it came with a worm.

68. This is a dreadful experience. Plus, now you have another hard choice to make: to wait out developments and recommit to the program or to leave the program, even though that may make you look flighty, undependable, and self-indulgent.

69. Like everyone, kirists hate this. They hate it that their life purpose choices may not pan out or pay off. They hate it that life can let them down. They hate it that life comes with such an opaque, distorting crystal ball. Who wouldn't hate this?

70. But they also know not to bash themselves for the thoughtful choices they make. If you step to the side before you make your choices, if you apply awareness to life, if you try your best to do the next right thing, why then bash yourself?

71. Our emotional health depends on us standing up for the idea of personally-designated life purpose choices; and accepting the results of the actual choices that we make, all subsequent shifting and all subsequent misadventures notwithstanding.

72. Maybe you're still inclined to reject this whole project. Your reasoning might go something like this: "If all I'm doing is nominating this and that as my life purposes, how valid or important is that? That's just me playing a pointless game."

73. "All I'm doing is saying that nothing really matters and trying to plug a leak in a sea of genuine nothingness. This is a game that I can see right through and I want no part

of it. Better to be lazy or mean or anything than to play this childish game!"

74. "No, who cares about my life purposes—me included. Why bother with these phony life purposes that I've elevated to some high-and-mighty place? Life is too hard, intractable and pointless for that and acting like I have purpose is pathetic."

75. There are many variations on this rejection. Some are angrier, some more despairing, some more anxious, some more ironic. We understand their power, logic, and, looked at one way, their validity. Kirists understand what is going on here.

76. Each variation amounts to the person announcing that if "life purpose" is only something that she herself gets to name, something without cosmic significance, just an idle claim that she makes, then it amounts to too little or even nothing at all.

77. But kirists recognize that this rejection is a hangover from the belief that life should be meaningful in some other deeper, more important sense, from the belief that it shouldn't just occasionally feel meaningful but actually be meaningful.

78. Life shouldn't just be organized around some purposes that I get to name, it should have purpose. If it is just this, then it is pathetic. Kirists understand the pull to reject the exact truth of the matter, that we're obliged to decide what's important.

79. Kirists learn to watch out for that quite reasonable, quite natural, and quite disturbing feeling, that their life purpose choices are only and just their life purpose choices

and not something more important than that or cosmically ordained.

80. Yes, a kirist will still sometimes see through this operation and remember that it is just he himself who has done the choosing. And yes, he will need strong, practiced rejoinders to the painful realization that life is exactly like this.

81. You can and must learn to accept that you intend to live a life based on your own calculations and that the universe doesn't care one way or the other. Likewise, you can and must learn how to respond to the truth that life is exactly like this.

82. What will your rejoinder be? "I don't need the cosmos to care. I care!" Or: "I may just be excited matter but I quite enjoy mattering, because I have plenty of good to do!" Or: "Every one of my life purposes makes perfect sense to me!"

83. Kirists even revel in the enterprise of naming and living their life purposes. Which of my life purposes shall I live today? Ah, what excellent choices! To love, to create, to serve, to right a wrong, to gain some mastery, to explore: what a lovely day!

84. You reject that pair of impertinent questions, "What is the meaning of life?" and "What is the purpose of life?" and you strive to answer the only really pertinent question, "How do I intend to live?" You shift the paradigm, all by yourself.

85. You make your list of your life purpose choices and you create your complementary life purpose statement. Then you use them. You hold the intention to live your life purposes and you actually live them on a daily basis. That is kirist living.

6

BOOK VI. TEMPESTS OF MEANING

1. Meaning comes and goes. That's its nature. Or rather, that's our nature. Sometimes we experience life as meaningful. Sometimes we don't. Just as sometimes we experience life as joyful and sometimes we don't. These are equivalent situations.

2. Why does meaninglessness hurt so much? Because it is the "feeling" equivalent of the thought, "Nothing matters." We say, "This meeting is so boring!", move to calling life a cheat and our life ridiculous, and pain floods in through that open door.

3. For how long can we just fill up time? For some people, forever! For others, not even ten minutes. Some people are keenly aware of the presence and the absence of the feeling of meaning. If you are one of those, a crisis is always brewing!

4. Our species can be rightly divided into two groups, those who take existence for granted and those who question the

nature of existence. The second group never rests. More self-pestering about the purpose of life! When, in fact, there are only choices.

5. Why can the tiniest thing make a day and the tiniest thing ruin a day? Because we are always calculating how life is going and the smallest thing can tip that calculation one way or the other. This existential brinksmanship is the great silent stressor.

6. Four people are sitting around a restaurant table, chatting and seeming happy. They get up—and each is immediately sad. What happened? The comfort of sociability abruptly ended and a strong whiff of meaninglessness returned.

7. There are answers to the question, "Can I experience life as meaningful?" But there is no salvation. You can live your life experiencing meaning but you still aren't saved. Salvation is the pipedream—crave it and you cultivate despair.

8. This moment passes. You evaluate it: "Boring." So, you make the leap: "Life is boring." Do you see how that leap is an unnecessary indulgence? You did not need to reevaluate all of life because of those five or ten or fifteen minutes!

9. Instinct is the enemy of the experience of meaning. That we betray our partner with an affair because of instinctual hunger is a meaning killer. But we are pathetically vulnerable—which means that we regularly kill off our own meaning.

10. You buy a book because its title calls to you in the place of meaning. Then you don't read it. Or you read it but it strikes you as slight and familiar. Did that sequence of hope and disappointment amount to a meaning wound?

11. It is that time of day. Maybe, 3 p.m. Meaning isn't holding. Doing the next right thing feels unbearable. Your body is ready to throw in the towel. You want to reach for some soothing, for oblivion, for an addiction. What to do?

12. When you say, "Nothing matters," you are also saying, "This doesn't matter." Whatever "this" is, you've robbed it of its power to produce meaning. You had an excellent intention, you said, "Nothing matters," and boom! You ruined now.

13. You claim that something is important to you. Say, it's writing. But you don't write. How likely are you to experience meaning if you aren't doing what you claim is important? How odd that you would expect meaning without honoring your intentions!

14. You cultivate the experience of meaning. You coax it. You try this and you try that. Sometimes you surrender, trying that as a tactic. You become a meaning tactician, a meaning strategist. You say, "Dark day. Trouble brewing. Let me try this!"

15. All you want to do is crawl into bed. And scream. And really not bother with all the ridiculous nonsense of living. Yes, you know about meaning coming and going—but it's gone now and you can't possibly "work on meaning." This is called despair.

16. You create a gorgeous thing. Maybe your best thing ever. Then you plummet into a deep hole, your deepest hole ever. Why all this pain on the heels of such a victory? Because beauty smells of mortality, just as ripeness smells of decay.

17. We would like at least some things to always feel meaningful. Shouldn't holding your child's hand never let you

down? But it sometimes will. That truth, however, is no indictment of hand-holding! Because, more often than not, it won't let you down.

18. What meaning opportunities are least likely to let you down? My list is short. Keeping quiet company with my wife. Pulling thoughts together. Family. Fighting the rising tide. Certain writers. Service of a particular sort. Corned beef.

19. I keep investing meaning in writing about meaning. That investment doesn't always pay off. Sometimes I'm too aware that I'm repeating myself. Sometimes I'm too aware that only a few people are listening. Sometimes it makes me dizzy. So be it.

20. What would be the height of maturity with respect to meaning? To not need it. To do the next right thing, and the next, whether or not it felt meaningful. To stop craving meaning and hating its absence. But what human can rise to such heights?

21. When we race around, we don't conceptualize that as flight. But often it is. Often it is flight from meaninglessness. To stop would be to smell the void. So, we rush around. But we smell the void anyway. It's in the air we breathe as we rush.

22. We are powerful and we are powerless. Sisyphus may smile but he is still tethered to a boulder. And for all eternity. Our powerlessness harms our ability to find life meaningful. How meaningful can life feel while tethered to a boulder?

23. Maybe it feels meaningful to support a certain candidate. Then you learn he's a toad. How could supporting

him still feel meaningful? You might still support him—but now, while feeling nauseous. Your reasons remain but not any feelings of meaning!

24. Which means: we have our reasons for doing things but the doing of them may not feel meaningful. We must accept that a percentage of our day is not going to feel very meaningful. But what if that percentage reaches 86% or 94%? How bleak is that!

25. But might 1% of meaning suffice? Or just 30 seconds? What if you had just a single experience of meaning on a given day, a brief shining heart tug in a sea of chores. Might that save the whole day? Might that justify existence? Might that be enough?

26. Say that you manage to encapsulate your many life purposes into a phrase of just a few words: for instance, "I do the next right thing." You now have your complete guidance. Hasn't meaning vanished as a problem? If only!

27. No, it didn't vanish as a problem. By accepting life as a project and by refusing to be made seasick by the tumbling waves of meaning and meaninglessness, you did calm the sea a bit. But more storms are coming. The storms keep coming.

28. On a really dreary day, can meaning hold? The pull is to slide toward "Nothing matters" and "Why bother?" Toward "Life is a cheat" and "I've been wronged." Toward "It's all too much" and "Screw it!" What a steep slide, all in an instant!

29. How can you do the next right thing if you don't believe in what you're doing? You used to believe in teaching anthropology—but no more. You used to believe

in the beauty of numbers—but no more. So, now you have neither purpose nor meaning. Ouch!

30. So, should you look to new purpose or to new meaning? You could go either way, couldn't you? You could announce, "Let me try this on as a new purpose." Or, "Let me make a meaning investment here and see what happens." Either is a reasonable effort!

31. But how was it that meaning drained out of anthropology or numbers? How did our experience of something change so radically over time that the thing lost its existential cachet? How can something be worth everything and then nothing?

32. I loved "the novel." I loved reading them and writing them. Then, over the course of forty years, I stopped believing in its importance. I wasn't down on it or angry with it, as if it had failed me. Rather, its importance got rejiggered.

33. Reality rejiggers. You see teaching children as an admirable life purpose. Then comes the world of tests, principals, colleagues, parents, and a loss of innocence. The ideal falls hard to the real. Teaching becomes a struggle. Meaning crisis!

34. Or perhaps meaning does hold. Hurrah! You love teaching from the day you start until the day you retire. What a blessing and lucky accident, that the place where you invested meaning paid lifelong dividends. What a blessing and how lucky!

35. Must so much—our whole life really—rest on accidents of good luck, like loving teaching from beginning to end? It looks as if it just might. You audition as an actor. You

win no auditions. No luck strikes. How can meaning possibly hold?

36. You keep trying. You say, "I'm not giving up." You say, "I feel terrible right now but it will get better." You say, "I matter and my efforts matter." You say, "I love myself completely." Still, nothing lucky happens. How can meaning possibly hold?

37. And maybe you didn't help luck along all that much. Maybe you didn't do everything you should have. Maybe you botched this and made a mess of that. Now you have that pain to reckon with, too, that further meaning drain. Is meaning holding?

38. "Meaning" is a subjective psychological experience. It's a plus or minus feeling about life's value. Who you are, what you've done, what's been done to you, how you think, all of that matters. A pratfall a long twenty years ago—and a meaning crisis now!

39. And what if you were seriously harmed in the bosom of your family? Don't we see people harmed that way and robbed of joy? Robbed of spontaneity? Robbed of life? What if you got robbed of the ability to experience life as meaningful?

40. You start with a huge repertoire of psychological experiences. You are curious. A slap eliminates that. You speak your mind. A yell and you're silenced. One by one, the experiences that might have made life feel meaningful are chased out of you.

41. Or maybe you rebel and embark on a wild ride. Still, nothing feels meaningful. That bit of sex. Nothing. That drug. Nothing. The sharpest point, the craziest antic: noth-

ing. You were harmed and now you're chasing a feeling that is not available.

42. Exactly this is at the root of the confusion between "searching for meaning" and hungering for a feeling. Meaning is not a pot of gold to be located. It's nowhere! You can't search for it, any more than you can search for awe or wonder. Impossible!

43. The night sky isn't awesome or wonderful. It's just the night sky. But you might experience something as you look up at it. You might go outside to have an experience. But the night sky did nothing. Something welled up inside of you —or it didn't.

44. You didn't go outside searching. You went outside hoping, anticipating, and hazarding a guess, based on your history of meaningful experiences. Just as you hazard a guess that you might love teaching, baking bread, or having children.

45. Stop searching for meaning, looking for meaning, or trying to find meaning, as if meaning was hiding under a bushel or got lost when you changed jackets. No guru has got it in his pocket or his podcast. But you've known that all along!

46. Instead say, "I understand meaning. It comes and goes. It's just what it is. It may prove elusive and it may even get lost for weeks and months on end. But my understanding of it is firm! I know exactly what it is, this strange, quixotic human feeling!"

47. And you possess tactics for coaxing it into existence. For one, you do things that once felt meaningful—maybe they'll prove meaningful again. Maybe you'll read that

book you once loved and see what you feel. Maybe meaning will well right up!

48. And you'll try things with a likelihood of feeling meaningful. You'll try being of service. That has a chance. You'll try fighting for a cause. That has a chance. You'll try walking by the ocean. That has a chance. Consult your list of meaning opportunities!

49. But you won't go seeking meaning, as if it could be found at the top of some mountain. To seek meaning is to not face life. The project of your life is defeated by a search for meaning. You may be able to coax meaning into existence but stop hunting for it!

50. You can live your life purposes right now and you can do the next right thing right now, but only if you are here right now, living the project of your life. You can rush off to Paris, if you like, but don't go hoping that Paris is where meaning resides!

51. The fruitless search for meaning is a hunt for reasons to believe that there is something "more" than ordinary life, a hunt for some secret something that would prove that we cosmically matter. Yes, we matter—just not to the universe.

52. Let the universe laugh at that, if it likes. Ah, but it has no way of laughing. So, no need to plug our ears to defend ourselves against that laughter. We are no cosmic joke. There is only vast, eternal silence there—and our life here.

53. Maybe you crave excellent reasons for accepting your human lot. Maybe you pine for a secret explanation as to why we're here, what purpose we serve as a species, and what purpose you serve as an individual. Let that go. Just stand up instead.

54. You say that you aren't experiencing meaning. But how could that possibly reduce your responsibility to do the next right thing? Did tyranny suddenly vanish? Did cruelty? Did misery? Warrior, forget about meaning! Stand up instead.

55. Universal meaning is an authoritarian idea. Personal, subjective meaning is a democratic idea. Authoritarians are happy to tell you what to believe. They say they have information right from the source of all things. But isn't that just a version of bullying?

56. To start a sentence with "The meaning of life is" is to betray our common humanity. To start a sentence with "The purpose of life is" is the same betrayal. How dare anyone try to bend all life purposes to their will. Completely unacceptable!

57. But what if you've been harmed and robbed of the ability to experience life as meaningful? You make an effort, you hazard a guess, you try this, you try that, but your efforts don't pay off. How demoralizing! Is there anything to be done?

58. Yes. Currently a psychological experience isn't available to you. But your thoughts still are. You can think your way to a good life. You can say, "Living with purpose is plenty and maybe the experience of meaning will follow." You can do that!

59. But what if you can't identify your life purposes because nothing feels important enough to qualify? Then you must announce, "I deem this and that important, even though they don't feel important." That is an odd game, but it is the right game.

60. And look, meaning is holding! For three straight weeks

you've been smiling, or smiling a bit. Then comes a terrible blow. You learn that your mate is cheating on you. You learn that your company wants to move you to a desolate country. What then?

61. Or maybe your freedoms are abruptly curtailed. Or you're diagnosed with an illness. Or your rent increases and you can no longer afford your apartment. Or your industry vanishes to technology and automation. In each case … what then?

62. Then you must deal with that crisis and you must also repair meaning. You undergo radiation or you make a career change and you also repair meaning. The fabric got ripped and you pull out your needle and thread and stitch meaning back together.

63. You repair it by reminding yourself that meaning is a wellspring that can and will return. That, even with your life purposes rejiggered, you are not bereft of purpose. That, this blow notwithstanding, you don't have to evaluate life as worthless.

64. It is a sunny day. You feel spirited. You feel alive. You even feel lucky. You are so tempted to exclaim, "Life is meaningful!" But you know better. You know that life isn't meaningful or not meaningful. Rather, you are having one lucky day of meaning!

65. And, yes, one lucky day of meaning can be followed by another. You are enjoying what you are doing. You are enjoying life. Plus, you are doing all the hard things, those life purpose choices that require heavy lifting. So, meaning is settled now, right? Ha!

66. A woman came up to me after a talk I gave. "Making meaning is just a game," she said, "one that I can see right

through." "Yes," I replied, "but it's the best game in town." Indeed, the void is always there. But so is the prospect of personal responsibility.

67. No matter what, our life remains our project. We can do good—or not. We can stand up—or not. We can think deeply—or not. We can care—or not. We can love—or not. Don't blame the universe if we opt for purposelessness. That's on us.

68. Do you have permission to throw in the towel? Well, who's to say otherwise? You have no personal services contract with the universe. But the choice to throw in the towel won't make you proud. At the last instant, you'll whisper, "I'm better than this."

69. But, how to release the heaviness? The despair? The anxiety? The emptiness? The anger? You do it by saying, "I do the next right thing, despite what I know about the universe and despite how I'm feeling." Can you do that amazing, difficult thing?

70. You are not taking a stand for or against the universe. You are taking a stand as a human being. You are saying, "I buy the idea of personal dignity." The universe won't care that you made that decision. But won't you?

71. Meaning is a wellspring and renewable resource. If your tire is flat, you patch it or you replace it. If your career is flat, you reinvest meaning in it or you start a new career. You don't say, "Meaning is gone for all time." That's a huge mistake.

72. The thought, "Meaning is gone for all time," invites despair. It creates a deep hole and, when you fall into that hole, how hard it is to get out again! Now nothing feels

worth doing. What an effort even to remove your socks! So, you sleep in your clothes.

73. Climbing out of that hole seems impossible. Yes, the sun is shining high above. But how does that help you? Who cares that it is beautiful up there? Down in that hole it is miserable. If the hole were a physical thing, you would never get out of it.

74. But it is psychological. And ladders appear in the darkness. Is love a ladder out? Is helping a child? Is fighting evil? A ladder appears—will you climb up it? Or are you too demoralized for that? Maybe today you are. But what about tomorrow?

75. Remember when you were nine, sitting in a comfy chair in a silent room, reading a book that moved you? That is no false memory. That can't be disputed or deconstructed. That was a meaningful experience. And if a child can have it …

76. Ah, but you and I know too much now, don't we? There is too much water under the bridge. Too many disappointments, too much that didn't pan out, too few beautiful dreams left. And such a vast sea of mundanity all around us …

77. Tease out of that sea of mundanity the three or five or seven or nine important things, the things of this moment or of all time, that you recognize as important or anoint as important. Do they not really feel important? Then anoint them as important!

78. In the silence that ensues, even as you can see the game you are playing, even as you can hear the laughter, you decide to matter. Call it absurd, call it comical, but that is

still the right answer: even as you smell emptiness, you ratify human dignity.

79. You live the project of your life. If it turns out that you are eternal, lovely. If the universe is smiling down on you, lovely. And if there is nothing, so be it. Forget the universe, forget the indignity, and say, "I do the next right thing. That's my choice."

80. If the polar ice caps melt, your life is still your project. If bullies appear on all sides, ruining everything, your life is still your project. You are a resistance fighter in the battle for human dignity. Yes, you could collaborate with nothingness. But don't!

81. And sometimes you'll experience meaning. How will that feel? Like pure joy? Like a piercing? Like wistfulness? Like the sea surging through you? Like understanding? Well, that feeling will pass. And the project of your life will continue.

82. Even if someone foretells your fate, the project of your life continues. Whatever those tea leaves, Tarot cards, or natal charts say, the project of your life continues. Whatever is or isn't or ever will be, the project of your life continues.

83. We are very accustomed to words like anxiety, depression, and addiction. We need a new vocabulary made up of phrases like meaning opportunities, meaning investments, meaning leaks, meaning drains, and meaning substitutes. And meaning crises!

84. With that new vocabulary, desperate dramas of seeking would end. No need to flee meaninglessness, as if it were a monster, or chase after it, as if it were the holy grail. You

would settle in and live, happy, despairing, anxious, calm and all the rest.

85. What is meaning? Just a sometimes constant, sometimes occasional, sometimes absent feeling, just an odd, everyday human thing. Meaning comes and goes; and through all that cataclysmic shifting, you can live a life of purpose, if you will.

7

BOOK VII. LIFE AS CHEAT

1. Why might you not feel equal to radical self-authorship? Maybe your personality needs an upgrade. Maybe your circumstances are dire. Maybe your thoughts are fighting with you. Or maybe you've decided that life is a cheat.

2. Many people have decided, quite consciously or just out of conscious awareness, that life has cheated them. It dropped them into a mean family. It gave them less than stellar looks. It set them up for a hard life leading inevitably to death.

3. This evaluation of life as a cheat is typically not a constant evaluation. We don't feel this way about life every single minute. For portions of the day we smile, amuse ourselves, and feel fine. Then darkness suddenly strikes, just like that.

4. The moment before we were laughing. Now we feel as cold as ice. We're likely to call this "depression." We may think that we need a therapist or a pill. What we really

need is to answer the question, "If life has cheated me, then what?"

5. What are some possible answers? Well, first is a rejection of the premise. "No, life has not cheated me. In order for it to have cheated me, it first needed to promise me something. But nothing was promised. So, no fraud was committed."

6. I wasn't promised good teeth. I wasn't promised the upper classes. I wasn't promised serenity. I wasn't promised decent parents. So, as I wasn't promised anything, I haven't been cheated. I am challenged, not cheated, which is different.

7. Or you might reject the language. "Is 'cheat' the right word? Or is it closer to 'disappointed'? 'Cheat' is such a big word, so hard to bear, so demoralizing! But 'disappointed'—well, maybe I can deal with that. Who doesn't get disappointed?"

8. Really, who doesn't get disappointed? It starts so early, the disappointments. Hoping for a kind word and getting criticism instead. Hoping to win and coming in last. Disappointments inevitably mount up. But that is different from being cheated.

9. Or you might evaluate life more generously. You might say, "Well, yes, I can list all the blows, all the indignities, and all the disappointments. But there was also some beauty and some goodness and some happiness and some victories."

10. You might shine a light on what is good and what is possible and what is available. This positive attitude is a decision you make to notice life's warm bits, despite all the

coldness. You say, "I choose to be a little bit upbeat, despite everything."

11. Or you might decide that you haven't been cheated at all. This might sound like: "I am free enough to live my life purposes, to tackle the project of my life, to find a measure of happiness, and to make myself proud. Where was I cheated?"

12. You had better do one of these or something similar or risk ruining your chances of ever experiencing life as meaningful. As long as "life has cheated me" remains stuck in your craw, you will feel that choking sensation as you choke on life.

13. Consider. Say that an experience did feel meaningful. Might you nevertheless denounce it as fraudulent? Yes, you might. It is completely possible to experience something as meaningful and then announce that it was not meaningful.

14. Or, say that an upcoming experience had the potential to feel meaningful. Might you actively prevent it from yielding that potential? Yes, by holding the conviction that, since life has cheated you, upcoming experiences can't possibly matter.

15. We regularly refuse to allow experiences to feel meaningful and we regularly reject as meaningful experiences that felt meaningful. Why do we pull the pin on meaning even as we say that we crave it and would do anything to secure it?

16. We do this because we've evaluated life as a cheat. We believe that life has somehow failed us and so we stop believing in the possibility of meaning. We may not be aware that we have done this but it's quite likely that we have.

17. Why might we not credit an experience as meaningful, even if we experienced it as such? The culprit is our evaluation of life. We've evaluated life as meaningless and a cheat. That evaluation forces us to label all experiences as meaningless.

18. So, despairingly, we do just that, even if we experienced the moment as meaningful. This tragic artifact of consciousness, that we are conscious of life not being just or measuring up, strikes even as we sit in the sunshine, having a good moment.

19. What could be more insidious? You chat with a child. It is enjoyable. It is more than that. It moves you. Then, as you walk away, you mutter, "Well, that was nothing special." By habitually calling everything nothing, you make them nothing.

20. Or maybe you stop to add your name to a petition to put a candidate on the ballot. For a split second, you have a tiny belief in political action. Then you mutter, "Well, that was ridiculous." Again, you turned something into nothing.

21. No experience can be credited as meaningful, even it if felt meaningful, to someone who has decided that life is meaningless. Every upcoming experience is already rendered meaningless to someone who has evaluated life as a cheat.

22. Say that, because you've experienced too much pain or been disappointed too often, you decide that nothing in life can ever feel genuinely enjoyable. As a result, you instantly sour experiences that might have felt joyful, raining on your own parade.

23. You ruin your chances for meaning by looking around and sighing, "Is this all there is? Really?" Or maybe you

say, “Life is ridiculous and pathetic, and, to top it off, supremely hard. What a stupid game!” More meaning ruined.

24. How we evaluate life matters. We experience life against the backdrop of our evaluation of life. If that evaluation is negative, nothing has much of a chance of feeling positive. Isn’t depression just a persistent negative evaluation of life?

25. Why might you evaluate life that harshly? Maybe because you went unloved as a child. Maybe because you’ve spent a stupendous amount of your time just earning a living. Maybe because you see immorality rewarded. So many reasons!

26. Maybe you had dreams that never materialized and goals that you never reached. Maybe you had expected more out of life—more from it, more from others, and more from yourself. Maybe … this list is extremely long, isn’t it?

27. It is easy and maybe even inevitable to evaluate life as a cheat, maybe easier and more likely than evaluating it as worth the candle. But how many unfortunate consequences flow from that decision and from that negative evaluation!

28. Is such an evaluation incorrect? Maybe not. How can any life that comes with pain and sorrow and that ends in death not be judged a cheat? How can any life that comes with strange dreams and pestering thoughts not be judged harshly?

29. What other evaluation is possible? So, maybe you’ve appraised life correctly. But that is only the beginning of

the conversation, not the end. Millions take it as the end of the story when it is only the beginning. Only the beginning!

30. This negative evaluation is only a bit of bedrock reality upon which you build your intentional life. Maybe you've appraised life correctly and there will be pain and there will be death and you'll only get 6% of what you want. Maybe that's true.

31. But, by taking that as the starting point and not as the end point, you pave the way to personal meaning. You say, with amazing modesty and with deep philosophical calm, "I have my serious work to get done as a principled human being."

32. You opt for modesty. How charming can a sweet cottage feel if you had it in mind that you were supposed to live in a castle? With mature modesty come countless lovely moments that would have eluded your more grandiose self.

33. For we are indeed grandiose. That grandiosity harms us. How much meaning or pleasure can you extract from writing a workmanlike paragraph of prose if you had it in mind that you were supposed to write bestsellers and become famous?

34. How much meaning or pleasure can you extract from chatting with a friend if you had it in mind that you were supposed to be the center of a whirlwind of attention? That lovely chat gets swamped by rolling waves of unhealthy narcissism.

35. Modesty is a key. But to be modest doesn't mean to settle. Not at all! There is no reason why the project of your life shouldn't include ambition, desire, and everything

else that nature has programmed you to crave. No settling needed!

36. First, you pull back the curtain to see if you've evaluated life negatively. This can feel like ripping off a bandage. It can hurt terribly to learn that you feel this way. Maybe you'll want to scream, "Life has cheated me! I didn't know I felt that way!"

37. Maybe you really didn't know. Maybe you're a software engineer, you write code day and night, you are well-paid and widely wanted, and the world is your oyster. Might you be holding life as a cheat despite all that? You might!

38. Maybe in those moments between code-writing thrills, when consciousness finds itself tumbling toward nothingness, when some original sadness comes back to haunt you, you arrive at an unconscious conclusion: I've been cheated!

39. Now, as a kirist, you make that evaluation conscious. If we wall off knowledge that upsets us, we fail to know that we have evaluated life as a fraud. Maybe we haven't evaluated it that way and that would be splendid. But maybe we have!

40. So, now we bravely look. Shouldn't we have gotten obvious clues from our behaviors? But we are very practiced at not looking in the mirror, so we didn't quite notice that we were living with agitation and despair. Now we notice.

41. All that pointless drinking. All those escapades. All that sex with strangers. All that muffled sobbing. All that Net surfing. All that tossing and turning. Did we not see that something had to be going on beneath the surface? No, we didn't.

42. Maybe you had glimpses. Maybe you came to negative conclusions about life but, supposing that it would do you no good to notice, or because you were just too embarrassed to admit it, you denied that you'd given life a thumb's down.

43. But you had. And that negative evaluation couldn't help but color everything. It colored your commute. It colored your free time. It made creating difficult. It made loving difficult. It made laughing difficult. It colored absolutely everything.

44. Now you can face that truth, that you consider life a cheat, and move on. Now you can say, "Well, it looks like I've concluded that life has cheated me. Let me say that as clearly and as openly as I can and get on with the project of my life!"

45. Evaluate life harshly, if you must. But leap right to the next step. Shout, "So be it! Here I am and I refuse to throw in the towel. I intend to live my life in a principled way, doing one right thing after another, to the best of my ability. Boom!"

46. Even though you may have ample reasons to feel that life is a cheat, you must, for the sake of experiencing meaning, for the sake of your emotional well-being, and because of some core moral imperative, move past that negative evaluation.

47. You announce, "Life may be a cheat, for which I have ample evidence. But despite being burdened with this absurd hand to play, I see a way to play it. I see what I can do today and I see what I can do tomorrow and I see how to live as a kirist."

48. You counter your calculations about life with a dedica-

tion to your life as project. You make this leap even though you've been harmed, even though you've been badly disappointed, even though you find life taxing and unrewarding. You leap.

49. Because you know that how you evaluate life colors how you perceive your experiences, you attempt the odd work of thoughtfully deciding if you can evaluate life more positively. Maybe, just maybe, a more positive evaluation is possible.

50. And if it isn't possible, you sigh and shrug. You say, "Sorry, life is a damned cheat. That's the fact of the matter. And I had better deal with that reality as best as I can, following the guiding principles of self-obligation and self-authorship."

51. You live your intentional life. And you keep checking for signs that your negative evaluation of life is creeping back in and undermining your efforts. You look for clues, which may be abundant, because that evaluation has a way of returning.

52. You check for a lack of motivation. If you feel unmotivated, you sit right up and exclaim, "Uh-oh. What's going on here? Am I down on life again? Have I somehow forgotten that, even if I am down on life, I'm obliged to do the next right thing?"

53. You check to see if you're despairing. Nowadays we call that "depression" and hope that a pill will make some difference. But you are wiser than that and say, "Hm, I'm very sad. Is that my feeling that life has cheated me coming back full bore?"

54. Maybe a compulsion has gotten hold of you. Maybe your drinking has gotten out of hand or maybe you feel in

the grip of something you can't name or escape. Check in. You may be running like mad from the feeling that life has failed you.

55. This checking in helps remind you that you refuse to be paralyzed by your sense of how life ought to be. That life ought to be fairer, that life ought to easier, that life ought to be rosier, must not stop you from living life intentionally.

56. Be careful of those "oughts" in your thinking. Yes, maybe your artwork ought to have been widely praised. Yes, maybe you ought to have been recognized. Yes, maybe you ought to be famous. Be careful! Those "oughts" are poison darts!

57. You remove their venom by saying, "What's next?" The project of your life must continue. It must continue despite your negative evaluation of life, despite your sense that life ought to be different, despite your grieving.

58. It would be lovely if your evaluation of life were, "Life is just fine and dandy!" But if that isn't your honest feeling, if in fact you see life as pointless, unfulfilling, even ridiculous, that negative evaluation must not be allowed to end the story.

59. Can you do that? Can you do something that amounts to your highest reach, the reach to pull yourself up when you don't feel good about life? You know why to do it. But can you do it? Can you "transcend" your evaluation and opt to care?

60. Can you manage to care? Can you manage to care about humanity when humanity doesn't care about you? Can you manage to care about justice when justice doesn't care about you? Can you manage to care if the caring isn't reciprocated?

61. Can you manage to care? Can you manage to care about this frail species, this flawed species, this vicious species, this unrepentant species, this dangerous species, maybe just for the sake of one child whose name you don't even know?

62. Can you manage to care? Can you manage to care when caring is tiring? Can you manage to care when caring is a nuisance? Can you manage to care when caring provokes the wrath of your neighbors? Are you up for this heroism?

63. You know why to do it. You know that meaning will elude you if you don't. You know that you'll feel adrift if you don't. You know that you won't respect yourself if you don't. You know why to do it. But can you do it? That's a real question.

64. You could just exclaim, "Life is a cheat. It will rob me of loved ones. It will rob me of myself, and for all eternity. It refuses to provide me with enough meaning or even with any meaning. It just makes work for me and brings me pain. Damn it!"

65. Or you could paint this other picture, the kirist picture, a picture of a lone human being calmly answering the call to be good, on his or her own terms, in the face of everything, knowing that everything is a lot and maybe too much.

66. You acknowledge your evaluation of life, whatever that evaluation may be, and you put that evaluation off to one side, so far off that it doesn't color your days, so far off that it hardly matters what that evaluation is. Off to the attic with it!

67. You treat your life as a project, an opportunity to make

yourself proud, and an adventure foisted upon you by nature. You hold your conception of how you intend to live as more important than your evaluation of life as positive or negative.

68. Indeed, maybe you're only down on life a little or only sometimes. Maybe you've judged life a six or a seven and not a zero. That will make your work easier! But easy or hard, the work remains, the work of doing the next right thing.

69. Yes, you may have been cheated. Maybe you were cheated in the looks department and you aren't comely. That must not prevent you from doing the next right thing. You don't want to sulk petulantly, as you know better than to do that.

70. Maybe you did some excellent research and someone stole your glory. You could have been Newton, Darwin, Einstein! But they robbed you. Do you want to grieve that for all eternity or move on and live? You know the right answer.

71. Maybe your parents were mean to you. You didn't deserve that, you hate that, and it colors everything. But aren't you obliged to author your own story in ways that make sense to you and that serve you, despite that terrible backstory?

72. Maybe you were born into a despised minority. That must be counted as cheating of the first order, mustn't it? So much pain and suffering right from the moment of birth and year after year thereafter. But, now … how shall you live?

73. You must tolerate your negative evaluation and live richly. Consider the alternative: to not be able to tolerate it

and to remain in a funk, sick to your stomach, half-ruined and holed up in an alley or living half a life. Consider that alternative.

74. It is such a self-kindness to sigh and say, "Yes, I genuinely feel this way, that life has failed me, but my head and my heart tell me that isn't the end of the story. I can still live my many life purposes, which would make me happy and proud."

75. Hate life, if you must. Live with permafrost, if you must. Hold a massive grudge, if you must. Judge that you've been treated unfairly, if that's your calculation. Then do just one additional thing: do not allow any of that to be the end of the story.

76. I've been telling my grandkids about Joe the Apple, who, instead of hanging on his tree, drops down, walks off, and has adventures. They cheer him on and understand completely. Hanging from that tree is just the beginning of the story!

77. It is an act of genuine self-kindness to air your grievances against life and then get on with the business of living. By moving on, you trade the ice-coldness of grievance for the warmth of effort and the heat of life.

78. Billions of people are unwittingly holding a grudge against life. Some act it out in bar fights, some criticize everything, some shut down and live half-hearted versions of the life they might have lived. Paint a picture for them of another way to live.

79. They unconsciously suppose that denying their grudge is the answer. It isn't. The answer is to announce what they feel, let the venom drain, make some peace with the

painful facts of existence, and opt for a kirist life of self-commitment.

80. Raging at the facts of existence is not the answer. Nor is despairing. You shift your gaze away from how life ought to be and you focus on the imperative, rising up in you from your own sources of good, to proudly contribute.

81. If life looks rosy to you, that is wonderful and amazing. If it looks rocky to you, if you feel half-ruined by circumstance, if you hate the hand you've been dealt, announce that loudly and clearly and shout, "But that is not the end of the story!"

82. We are burdened by many powerful reasons not to bother. One of those powerful reasons is our sense that life is not a fair game. We throw up our hands and exclaim, "I will not play this rigged game!" But doesn't that gesture feel terrible?

83. Maybe you can find no way to convince yourself that life matters. But that is not the end of the discussion. You move right along and decide that your efforts matter, whether or not life matters. That is the kirist leap: your efforts matter.

84. Is it absurd to affirm that your efforts matter? Perhaps. But if it is absurd, you simply laugh and say, "I'm comfortable with absurdity." You say, "I take this life as an obligation of a certain sort, no matter how ridiculous that may be."

85. You say, "My life is my project and I accept that absurd, unglamorous, heroic task. I am not really up to being a hero but so be it. I accept." You do not let your sense that life is a cheat stop you from fulfilling your obligations to yourself.

8

BOOK VIII. DYNAMIC INDWELLING

1. A useful philosophy of life should include a sensible philosophy of mind. We are what we think and we are obliged to get a grip on our own mind. This is a core self-obligation and a necessary task if we mean to engage in genuine self-authorship.

2. Philosophers from Marcus Aurelius to the Buddha have announced this as a top priority. Cognitive-behavioral therapy is the modern way that this age-old message is delivered. But so far none have offered an accurate enough picture of mind.

3. The ways that we've been invited to get a grip on our mind, whether those invitations come from traditions like Stoicism or Buddhism or from cognitive-behavioral therapists, fall short because they do not accurately picture our inner dynamism.

4. A major shortcoming of past philosophies and psychologies is that they do not speak to what it really feels like to have a mind. We do not just "have thoughts." Rather, we

indwell dynamically in what we'll dub "the room that is our mind."

5. We live in the room that is our mind. That is where we live, rather than in San Francisco, Berlin or Bangkok. That is where we spend our waking and sleeping hours. Your mood is made there, your intentions are set there, and your life is lived there.

6. Descartes pictured that indwelling place as a stage where we play out our dramas. But Descartes' image paints a picture of us more as observers than as dramatists and actors. In the room that is our mind, we create our own dramas and play them out.

7. Our mind is a "real" place where we dwell. It is sometimes a comfortable place and sometimes a tortured place. But it is first of all a place, amorphous, ambiguous, but real. We spend our time there and acquire or create our particular indwelling style.

8. That style then affects everything that we do and that we are, from the way we present ourselves in the world, called our personality, to the way that we experience inner states with names like "happiness," "depression," "mania," and "anxiety."

9. Some acquire a needling style, needling themselves as they think. Some acquire a critical style, creating criticisms rather than thoughts. Some acquire a muffled style, where thoughts never get fully formed. There are many indwelling styles.

10. Some people always rage in there, even if they aren't raging in the world. Some are always sad in there, even if they put on a happy face in the world. Some are always

meek in there, even if they manage to function in the world. In there, you are you.

11. The atmosphere in there may feel claustrophobic. It may feel murky. It may make you queasy. Imagine opening the door to a steam room, a boiler room, or an auditorium filled with third-graders. Opening the door to the room that is your mind is like that.

12. The metaphor of "the room that is your mind" serves us. It is a useful concept and suggests how fundamental change can occur. A major personality upgrade is "spring cleaning" that room by choosing and creating your preferred indwelling style.

13. Our metaphor helps us better understand the idea of persona and how personality presents itself. We may live in the room that is our mind in one way, say angrily, and we may present ourselves in the world in quite another way, say placidly.

14. We may look confident in the world but be weak-kneed inside that room. We may look cheerful enough but be despairing in that room. We may look opinionated but not really believe our own opinions. We are one thing outside and another inside.

15. Our metaphor also suggests the sorts of activities that you might want to engage in. For instance, you might redecorate your room, you might air it out, you might let in some natural light, you might add closets, you might refurnish it, and so on.

16. If we want emotional health and if we're interested in self-authorship, our task is to make that room as comfortable a place as possible. If, say, our experience there is like

living on a bed of nails, how can we have the kirist life we're envisioning?

17. We can effect change there. A brain's true brilliance is in its ability to chat with itself, to enter into self-conversation, and, as a result, to engage in dynamic, system-wide self-regulation. Is anything in the universe more amazing than that?

18. We can chat with ourselves and we can aim ourselves in one direction or another, toward, for example, calmness versus anxiousness, passion versus indifference, love versus enmity, and so on. We are amazing, dynamic, self-regulating organisms.

19. Sitting on the easy chair that we our ourselves decide to install, we can go about the business of making decent sense of the contradictions that come with being human. First, though, we must get off of our bed of nails and drop into that easy chair.

20. What happens more usually when we enter? We're deluged with noise. Or it's as if a fog machine has gone wild and turned our inner world opaque. Or we're agitated in some way that renders it impossible to engage in smart self-regulation.

21. We typically do a poor job of self-regulation. We indulge thoughts that don't serve us and may even prefer to think that we can't self-regulate. However, that's just a shame and not an argument against the possibility of self-regulation.

22. We can do better. We can use our available freedom to indwell in ways that serve us. You can enter the room that is your mind not as a victim of consciousness but as a

talented creator equal to defining and designing what goes on in there.

23. Consider. Maybe you're drinking too much alcohol. Your cells adapt to your drinking habits and now they crave alcohol. You certainly have a "biological problem" and you may even have been born with a genetic predisposition. Biology plays its part.

24. Your unregulated mind likewise craves the anxiety relief of alcohol. You now have a "psychological issue" with respect to drinking and words like dependence, obsession, compulsion and addiction come into play. Psychology plays its part.

25. Maybe you also self-identify as a hard-drinking, passionate, rebellious type, revel in that identity, and see your drinking as a personality fit. Your self-identifications and formed personality help maintain the problem. Personality plays its part.

26. Maybe most of the adults in your family love to drink and you are caught up in a social dynamic that supports your drinking. There is alcohol everywhere, at every meal, at every party, at every function. Social dynamics play their part.

27. On top of all that, maybe your job is stressful, your children are acting out, your marriage is on the rocks and you drink to relieve all those stresses. Maybe your circumstances have worsened recently. Your circumstances play their part.

28. It's clear how these five—biology, psychology, personality, social pressures, and circumstances—are contributing to your problem drinking. If that were the end of the story,

we would have to say that those five were determinative. But they aren't.

29. That isn't the end of the story. If that were the end of the story, no one would ever get sober. But people do. They step to one side and engage in a self-conversation about sobriety. They consciously decide to self-regulate and to indwell differently.

30. A dynamic self-regulation model does not reject the biological, psychological, personality, social and circumstantial causes of thoughts, behaviors, moods and emotional distress. Rather, it rejects that we are just those things and not also conscious.

31. In that room, we can be conscious of consciousness. There we can be self-aware, if we cultivate an aware indwelling style. This odd feature of consciousness, that you can stand to one side, defines our species. There is a "you" that can know "you."

32. Seated comfortably in your easy chair, your room redecorated and your indwelling style improved, you can reduce your sadness, halt pestering thoughts, calm your nerves, eliminate unnecessary dramas, and improve your mental landscape.

33. But in order to pull off that feat, you must get rid of that bed of nails, install that easy chair, clean out those closets, let in some air, and all the rest. You must make a serious effort at spring cleaning and at redesign and redecoration.

34. Maybe even just adding some windows would help with those states with names like "depression, "anxiety," "obsessive-compulsive disorder," "mania" and even "schiz-

ophrenia." Who knows how beneficial it might be to just let in a little air?

35. How many times have you thought that same stale thought? How many times have you had that same tiring conversation with yourself? How much airless repetition can you possibly endure? Install some windows and throw them wide open!

36. What if you installed two windows, threw them open, and let a in cross breeze? Wouldn't some regrets waft away? Wouldn't some disappointments dissolve and disappear? Wouldn't you find a little peace without having to open another beer bottle?

37. The phrase "get a grip on your mind" suggests work. But how much heavy lifting is involved in installing a few windows? No trips needed to the hardware store. No chance of the glass not fitting the frames. Just picture them added and they are added.

38. Wouldn't everything change for the better, just the way that life changes for the better when a cloud passes and we see the sun again? Wouldn't a balmy breeze make you feel happier? Can you begin to see how you might employ this metaphor?

39. Who wants claustrophobia? Don't you want airiness, a breeze, and a blue sky? Don't you want concentration but while rocking in a hammock? Don't you want focus but while gazing out to sea? Doesn't adding windows sound like, well, a breeze?

40. Let's go a step further. Rather than just installing a few windows, let's picture your mind as a room with one side completely open to the sea breeze. In that mind of yours, the air is always circulating. Your thoughts are always fresh.

41. In that mind, stuffiness never accumulates. In that mind, new thoughts occur every day and old thoughts just waft away. Your formed personality created a room with no windows. Now you use your available personality to inaugurate a real remodel.

42. Your indwelling goals are to move from self-unfriendliness to self-advocacy, from self-opaqueness to self-awareness, from a learned passivity to a more native aliveness. Passive indwelling is the rule. Dynamic indwelling is the exception and the goal.

43. When you indwell dynamically, you get in the habit of not taking the thoughts that bubble up at face value. You stand in new relationship to them, inquiring of them, asking them to explain themselves, and learning to understand yourself.

44. For example, even a simple-sounding thought like "This café is crowded," is likely the culmination of a complicated internal conversation about which the thinker may be only half-aware or even entirely unaware. Many thoughts are like that.

45. Say that the thought "This café is crowded" is thought by a would-be writer who is struggling to write his novel, who doubts his ability to write his novel, and who most of the time finds excuses and reasons not to write his novel.

46. For him, the thought "This café is crowded" is not really a bit of objective appraising about the café but rather an excuse to not sit down and write. He thinks that thought, refuses to examine it or converse with it, and feels justified in leaving instantly.

47. When he gets to the next café, the thought that arises might be "This café is noisy," which will have arisen for

exactly the same reasons. When he gets to the third café, the thought might be, "Oh, I know too many people here!" Again, he leaves instantly.

48. Soon he may find himself drinking Scotch instead of working on his novel or hunting for sex instead of conjuring up answers to his novel's plot problems. By the end of such a disappointing day, isn't he likely to be filled to the brim with fury and despair?

49. Each of those thoughts about the cafés on his route sounded plausible enough: too busy, too noisy, too filled with familiars. But they were actually weaponized thoughts, weaponized by the thinker against himself. They weren't innocent at all.

50. It would have much better served that would-be writer to not react reflexively to the content of those thoughts but rather to ferret out their real significance and his underlying reasons for fleeing. We wish he'd stepped to one side and reflected.

51. That kirist step to one side allows consciousness to apply itself to consciousness. It transforms a passive indwelling style, where thoughts are accepted without reflection, to a dynamic style, where thoughts are treated as worth understanding.

52. Kirists use consciousness so as to be conscious. They say, "I intend not to live in the dark, as if no one had installed a bright light in my mind. I have turned on the light. I will not live in an unconscious or half-conscious way. I intend to know me."

53. We employ the metaphor of "the room that is our mind" to help us apply consciousness to consciousness. Our metaphor encourages us to see ourselves as active

investigators and lively creators of our mindspace and not as mere passive observers.

54. The very notion of entering that room implies activity. It suggests that there is a place we can visit where we can carry out smart conversations with ourselves. We do not need to live victimized by our thinking. We can take better charge than that.

55. You open that door and enter with energy. You look around. There is plenty to see and you see it all clearly, because you've installed overhead lighting, atmospheric lamps, and good-sized windows that allow in natural light and a soft breeze.

56. Our metaphor is at once serious and playful. It is serious in the sense that it allows for improved self-regulation and more dynamic indwelling. It is playful in the sense that you can be as whimsical and imaginative as you like in the way that you use it.

57. How whimsical and imaginative? You could install a speaker's corner where you speak your truth. You could install a safety valve that you use to reduce mental pressure. You could install a calmness switch that, when flipped on, produces instant calm.

58. You could add a resilience mat where you do your resilience exercises and recite your resilience vows. You could repaper those drab walls with cheerful wallpaper. You could add a fireplace and a blazing fire, for those cold days of the heart.

59. You could create a dresser with a deep hat drawer, fill it with hats of all descriptions, and pull out the hat that you want to wear next. Maybe it's the hat that matches the

mental task at hand or that helps put you in the mood you intend to nurture.

60. In that same dresser, you might create the drawer where you keep your corrective lenses, the ones you put on when your view of life seems fuzzy or distorted. You have other dresser drawers available, too. What might you put in those?

61. You might create a hope chest that you fill with objects, ideas, mementoes and talismans that help you keep hope alive. On hopeless days, you'd visit there, pluck out a postcard or a shining ideal, and feel at least a little bit more hopeful.

62. You might hang up a painting of a bowl filled with apricots, some of the apricots perfect, some bruised, and some rotten. Your painting is there to remind you how process works, that process comes with real messes as well as masterpieces.

63. Maybe you'll have some mattering t-shirts hanging in your closet, each emblazoned with a slogan like "I matter" and "My efforts matter." Maybe you'll include a grandeur corner, the spot you visit to remind yourself of the availability of grandeur.

64. You can design your room so that visiting there reduces your stress. You can design your room so that visiting there brings you some peace and quiet. You can design your room as a place where even the knottiest problems get unraveled.

65. Most people cultivate a passive indwelling style where thoughts arrive and are allowed to be thought uncontroverted. Out-of-sight, unexamined psychological processes

create those thoughts and the recipient passively accepts them as gospel.

66. Kirists, on the other hand, make the conscious decision to live in the room that is their mind more energetically, dynamically and thoughtfully than that. They learn how to be silent there, how to be calm there, and how to be productive there.

67. The room that is a person's mind is not some sort of optional accessory. It is the exact way that human consciousness is experienced. Kirists are obliged to concern themselves with its specific features, features like its airlessness or its spaciousness.

68. If it's hard to breathe in there, if it's hard to think in there, if it's hard to create silence in there, how well can we meet our self-obligations, champion our causes, make use of our potential, or author our story? How we indwell matters.

69. It may matter far more than we know. Our own significant contribution to any so-called mental disorder or other distress or disturbance we're experiencing may include the indwelling style we've cultivated over time and thoughtlessly adopted.

70. Cultivating an unfortunate indwelling style can turn that room into a painful place of conflicts, worries, fears, and other sufferings, so painful a place that we strenuously avoid going there and rarely do, rendering us dull and uncreative.

71. Or we may spend time there without quite noticing how miserable we feel when we're there. Our misery may go undetected and uninterrupted, supported by an

indwelling style that produces pain and then defensively muffles it.

72. Kirists understand this. They know that they have to take charge of cultivating an indwelling style of their own choosing if they are to have the life they want. They use their human-sized freedom to create right mindspace.

73. You can consciously design the room that is your mind, the place where you go to think, muse, imagine, problem-solve, daydream, and do everything mental. You can design it and you can make decisions about how you'll be when you visit there.

74. You can decide that you will be calm there. You can decide that you will be thoughtful there. You can decide that you will be brave there. You can decide that you will be passionate there. You can decide that you will be present there. You can decide.

75. You can be intense when intensity is called for, you can be calm when calmness is called for, and, with practice, you can be simultaneously calm and intense. Mightn't a calm-and-intense indwelling style serve you nicely?

76. You can lounge in your easy chair, as relaxed as can be, and at the same time tackle the intellectual intricacies of even the most challenging thought problem. Mightn't a relaxed-and-thoughtful indwelling style serve you nicely?

77. You can begin to make excellent sense of how you arrived there. Did you arrive of your own volition, which is a kirist goal, or instead because you were pulled by the nose by some internal conflict, pressing worry, or unproductive obsession?

78. You can likewise make excellent sense of how you want

to leave. You can leave all in a rush, hardly able to catch your breath, or you can leave in a more measured way, prepared to tackle some absurd rebellion or other self-obligation.

79. You can learn to discern when your mindspace has become overheated, when mania is threatened, when the activity of indwelling has become dangerous. You can learn to announce "This is getting dangerous!" so clearly that you hear yourself.

80. You can learn to spot when your indwelling style has darkened your mood. Maybe you've been conjuring up the idea that life is a cheat or that the past has ruined you. You throw open the back door and usher those thoughts right out.

81. You will have to deal with a lot, with strange musings, with insults not forgotten, with secrets that you're keeping from yourself, with whispers about impermanence and mortality. That you have installed an easy chair will not make this easy.

82. It requires real mind artistry to deal with all of that. Maybe you want to write novels or paint paintings and think that that's your main artistry. But mind artistry comes first. It's the talent that allows you to manifest your other talents.

83. As robust as the metaphor of "the room that is your mind" may be, it hardly captures everything that we might want to say about self-regulation, self- awareness, dynamic indwelling, and how consciousness can effectively oversee consciousness.

84. Still, it's a useful device. Kirists embrace the idea that their mind is a place that they can design and stylishly

inhabit. They replace the too-small idea that they are merely a thinker of thoughts with the larger idea that they can wisely self-regulate.

85. The activity of forthrightly dealing with one's inner reality in a now brightly-lit room is what we're calling dynamic indwelling. Dynamic indwelling is the number one self-regulatory tool that human beings possess and a centerpiece of kirist living.

9

BOOK IX. ETHICS AND GOODNESS

1. Kirists, who want to be good and who want to do good, learn that they must become full-fledged ethicists. To accomplish their heroic feats, they are obliged to look beyond black and white and make personal sense of complexity and ambiguity.

2. A kirist comes to recognize how her cherished values compete. She comprehends the nuanced differences between this current situation and a very similar past one. She sees the multiple sides of every moral argument. None of this is easy.

3. She sees that she must do the deciding. Absolute zero may be absolute but there are no absolute moral principles. She can't turn to a list or a rule book. She must turn matters over, even as life relentlessly rushes by, demanding that she decide.

4. Nor is her society likely to support her in her efforts. Society lays down strict, simple-to-say and simple-to-remember rules for its own convenience. No kirist will find

these self-serving, authoritarian rules very satisfactory or compelling.

5. A kirist will necessarily butt heads with these strict rules at every turn. Corporations have their rules. Schools have their rules. Families have their rules. Police departments have their rules. Even four women lunching together have their rules.

6. Every culture is rule-bound. These rules will tax her. If the rule is to never report bullying at work, how well will that sit? If the rule is to not talk back to authority, no matter how brutal authority acts, will she just nod? She will be a troubled ethicist.

7. If she loves fairness, justice, freedom and the other ideals of goodness, she will not fit comfortably into society. She may say nothing, she may hold her peace, but she won't be smiling. And won't the blues begin to haunt her?

8. Even a young kirist finds herself confronted by these challenges and confounded by this knowledge. Why should it be against the rules to talk back to her mean third grade teacher? But it is. What can she do except keep silent or speak and be punished?

9. In the fairy tales she reads, good triumphs. Life does not look like that. She wonders about that, she is confused by that, and she is hurt by that. And she can't help but notice her own dark shadows, those pockets of spite, those edges of intolerance.

10. Despite all this and more, kirists have no doubt where they stand. They stand with goodness. They intend to be good and to do good and they demand goodness from their society. As challenged as they feel, they are clear and adamant.

11. Kirists come to realize that while consciousness allows for apprehension of the good, it hardly guarantees that a person will do good. They see too much "not goodness" all around them, from bullying parents to punishing politicians.

12. They recognize that as a species, we are stuck with the reality of evil, both in ourselves and in others. They don't need to run through a litany of holocausts to be convinced. They see it every day, in the small interactions between human beings.

13. Maybe a future human being will evolve who is more ethical than us. While we wait on evolution, we must deal with who we precisely are. To begin with, we start out in a quagmire, because who is to adjudicate what is "right" and "wrong"?

14. Which is more ethically suspect, to patriotically fight in an immoral war, to support that war but to make sure that your son is exempt from duty, to flee the country so as not to have to fight in that war, or to blithely ignore that the war is going on?

15. Is it immoral to eat a cow? Is it immoral to write poetry while people starve? Is it immoral to choose a prestige profession that subtracts from our quality of life? These matters can't be adjudicated from on high, as there are no cosmic courts.

16. With your feet firmly mired in complexity and ambiguity, you must judge and you must decide. Words like "right" and "wrong" and "good" and "evil" drop us into a quagmire where kirists dwell. There is no way out for you and for me.

17. How can there be a way out when there is no earthly

way to rank competing values? Which is the higher value, compassion or self-protection? Which is the higher value, your life or my life? Which is the higher value, truth-telling or loyalty?

18. There is so much grayness. Why engage in whistle-blowing if that threatens your family? Why do another right thing when you've done several already? Haven't you been good enough today? What's to stop you from just watching a little television?

19. How are you to decide about anything? You love 25% of a candidate's views, you can tolerate 50% of his views, and you find 25% of his views intolerable. But he is better than any of the other candidates. Do you vote or sit out the election?

20. You are working on a new piece of technology. You can see its benefits and its drawbacks. You find yourself leaning toward not believing that it is a good thing for the world. But this is how you earn your living. Should you quit or keep at it?

21. There are many easy ways out of these moral dilemmas and they are all contemptible. One is to ruthlessly simplify. You turn the complexity of competing values into the simplicity of commandments. This is the authoritarian weapon of choice.

22. Authoritarians love the language of absolutes, which makes them more powerful than kirists. They can keep shouting "Love thy neighbor!" or some other slogan without meaning a word of it. Kirists do not allow themselves this hypocritical way out.

23. A kirist is obliged to be a full-fledged ethicist, which means that he is obliged to weigh and measure conflicting

values as they play themselves out in real life situations. This is absurd, taxing, and ultimately saddening. How could it not make one sad?

24. We accept the likelihood that our ethical decisions will come tinged with sadness. If you decide that you must never see a friend again, because his actions are reprehensible, are you also supposed to feel happy? Deciding is not some gleeful activity.

25. No doubt the thing called "depression" is supported by the difficulties we face in dealing with life's moral complexities and ambiguities. Those difficulties make us sad. We would like to be good and we are made sad by how competing values stymie us.

26. Is it good to provide your child with so many activities that he becomes very accomplished but has no childhood? What are the ramifications of that? Are you after a little Mozart or a little Einstein or a child who doesn't retch at the thought of school?

27. Is it good to accept all medical advice without question, to question every bit of it, or to somehow choose which to accept and which to reject? If the latter, how could you possibly go about such everlasting and inconclusive investigations?

28. You have an apprehension of the good, you want to be good, but which is the right way? Can there be a right way, given that values compete and that none are absolute? Or must we settle for our best efforts, aware that we are juggling imponderables?

29. And what about the pressure put on you by the powers that be, who are busy manipulating your views about right and wrong? If you need good information in order to

make an informed decision and the information you receive is false, what then?

30. Say that the consensus view, manipulated into existence, is that your child's fidgeting qualifies as a mental disorder. You are told that he ought to be drugged. Aren't you at real risk of believing that's the right path, since everyone is in agreement?

31. You are. Not only are ethical decisions made difficult because values compete and because real-life situations are complex and ambiguous, they are made even more difficult because the information we receive may not prove the least bit reliable.

32. All this makes us want to throw up our hands and shout, "The heck with goodness!" But we know that we mustn't. We know that would amount to a capitulation to darkness. We have plenty of reasons to throw in the ethical towel but we mustn't.

33. So, you try. But, harboring the wishful hope that trying is going to feel good, when it doesn't you may feel disappointed and that much less interested in ethical action. Kirists know to watch out for this trap, of needing ethical action to feel good.

34. Kirists strive not to be seduced by the notion that an ethical action ought to feel good. In fact, it may feel horrible and like the last thing on earth you want to do. Kirists are obliged to let go of craving that ethical actions will produce happy feelings.

35. Why might an ethical action feel horrible? Because ethical action can prove dangerous. Ethical action can prove confrontational. Ethical action can prove embarrass-

ing. And ethical action is always consequential. Ethical action is like that.

36. Maybe the rule in your community is to never speak up. But you see an injustice. Goodness requires that you break the community rule. You are not thrilled to break it or eager to break it. In fact, you may feel terrified. But your break it.

37. Maybe the law says that you're liable for the injuries you cause when you come to the aid of an accident victim. But, arriving at the scene of an accident, you decide to help. Goodness requires that you act, the law be damned. Reluctantly, you help.

38. Maybe it is a custom in your community not to work on Thursday. You find that custom arbitrary and unjustified and your family needs the income. So, you open your store on Thursday, certain that there will be massive repercussions.

39. Maybe you're positive that you ought to take your daughter to the upcoming father-daughter dance. But you know that dancing is going to embarrass you. Unhappy about looking foolish but determined to do the right thing, you go.

40. Maybe you've spent twenty years moving up the ladder in a prestigious profession. But over those years you've begin to discern that its practices are ethically shady. Although it is dramatically life-altering to leave that profession, you leave it.

41. In none of these scenarios is doing what you believe is right bringing you any joy whatsoever. Ethical action does not come with cartwheels. Nor is a single ethical action

likely the end of the story. Isn't it just as likely a link in a chain of ethical actions?

42. Very often a series of ethical actions is required, one leading to the next and each bringing its own pain and drama. At some point, a particular action may feel too difficult, too dangerous, or too unwise to pursue. And so, the process gets derailed.

43. I remember a moment in the Army. I was stationed in Korea and had been promoted to acting platoon sergeant. I began to feel strongly that accepting that rank made me more complicit in the raging Vietnam War than had my lower rank.

44. The action I took was to march into the company commander's office and demand that I be made a private again. I thought I was serious but the company commander took my demand to be a quixotic gesture, which perhaps it was. He laughed.

45. He said that he could certainly accommodate me but that it would require a court martial and some stockade time. I thought about that for a long moment and replied, "No thank you, sir." I remained a platoon sergeant for the rest of my tour.

46. These are the chimerical, weird, half-baked exercises in ethical acting that come with living. You take a stand—but you find that you can only take that stand for so long. You bravely put yourself out there—but only up to a point. Resolve melts away.

47. Doing the next right thing is one difficult thing and doing the right thing after that is another difficult thing. You may feel equal to the first but not equal to the second

or the third. You were brave and then you no longer felt so brave.

48. Maybe pushback from the first made the second that much harder. Maybe the effort involved in stepping to the plate that first time exhausted you. Maybe paltry results from the first made it more difficult to find motivation for the second.

49. A kirist recognizes this. He realizes that "doing the next right thing" may often amount to a never-ending string of actions and not to one stand-alone act of heroism. Standing up for civil rights, for instance, is not an event or a moment. It is forever.

50. There is a sighing that accompanies ethical action, a sighing that signifies that ethical action is difficult, complicated, opaque, and exhausting. It also signals that sometimes our actions result in tragic unintended consequences.

51. There is a terrible moment during World War II when the British navy sinks the fleet of their French ally. They do this to ensure that the French fleet will not fall into the hands of the Nazis. In the process, they kill thousands of French sailors.

52. Kirists think about this and sigh. They see what went into this. Hubris. Fear. Brinksmanship. Miscommunications. The fog of war. Rivalries. Chaos. Uncertainty. And they see what comes out of this, including, in this case, lifelong French enmity.

53. A kirist prepares herself for the ardors of ethical action. She discerns that she must be an historian, a language philosopher, a social scientist, and more. Since, in her peculiar way, she is responsible for the world, she needs to understand the world.

54. She trains herself to understand how language works. She comes to understand the linguistic power of a sentence like "God is good," why it can hold sway over billions of people, and how to defend herself and others against seductive grammar.

55. She comes to understand that just because something is a certain way, that isn't proof that it ought to be that way. She knows that "We do it this way" isn't legitimate justification for announcing, "Therefore it ought to be done this way."

56. She may not know that its technical name in formal philosophy is the "naturalistic fallacy," but she knows perfectly well not to make the leap from "what is" to "what ought to be." She can't be fooled in that way or persuaded in that way.

57. The main thing she learns is something she is already practicing as a kirist, namely that vital step to one side. In order to create the space necessary in which to reflect, calculate, and come to her wisest ethical conclusions, she steps to one side of the fray.

58. She may only spend a moment there, as her truest answer may arrive instantly. Or she may have to walk by the lake for an hour. Or she may have to sleep on the matter for several nights running. Or it may take her months of frustrating uncertainty.

59. Each ethical decision will come with its own time frame, its own rhythm, and its own difficulties. Why should it take a mere split second to know what to do if your teenage son decides to convert, enlist in the Marines, or marry his teenage girlfriend?

60. You step to one side, sigh, and ponder. You are stuck

knowing that there can't be a rule or principle to apply, as that would amount to believing that one particular value was primary. Rather, you know that ethics are situational and contextual.

61. A kirist doesn't hunt for some simple rule to apply. When it comes to ethical action, no rule is a replacement for reasoning. Rather, you step to one side, no matter how badly you are pressured to act, and thoughtfully turn the matter around.

62. Consider. You are the eldest daughter of a tyrannical mother who has gotten old but who is no less mean than she's always been. She is still demanding, blaming, shaming, and violent. And now she's also decrepit and in need of fulltime care.

63. The ironclad rule in your culture is that the eldest daughter takes care of the mother. The other siblings have no such obligations and can do as they please. You know that this is the rule and you know that this is what everyone expects of you.

64. What is the right thing to do in this situation? For a kirist, it can't be a mindless acceptance of a rule which just amounts to "Since this is what we do, it is the right thing to do." Blindly following such a cultural rule would amount to an abdication.

65. Instead of accepting the rule, you step to one side and think. You ask yourself, "Why shouldn't my brothers and sisters share in this load?" You ask yourself, "What is my exact obligation to a person who has always terrorized me?"

66. You ask yourself, "How guilty would I feel if I decide not to take care of my mother?" You ask yourself, "Might

breaking this authoritarian rule help some other women in my culture?" You step to one side, keep a mindful distance, and think.

67. You factor in reality. Would violating this rule prove easy? No. Might violating this rule prove very dangerous? Yes. Your bullying brother might beat you. The women in your culture might shun you. The men in your culture might curse you.

68. You factor in as much as you can. Might some of your siblings prove allies? Might some other relatives align with you? Has this rule ever been successfully broken? Is leaving your culture an option, and maybe even a necessity? You ponder.

69. After a minute, a day, or a month, you come to a conclusion. And when you decide, are you likely to feel sanguine about your decision? Of course not. How could you feel sanguine? There is so much difficult reality on either side of the equation!

70. Given the dangers involved, why would anyone ever violate such an iron-clad rule? Well, a kirist might, because she refuses to be tyrannized, because she believes her siblings ought to help, and because she is thinking about the welfare of others.

71. Thinking about the welfare of others is an aspect of kirist goodness. That goodness might sound like, "Maybe if I refuse to obey this rule, that will somehow help future generations of girls and spare them from having to follow oppressive rules."

72. She thinks about herself, about her particular situation, and about the competing values she is weighing. At the same time, she thinks about others, about how her actions

might support a better civilization, the general welfare, and goodness writ large.

73. That step to one side allows for reflection and awareness. But it is also a step for humanity. It is a vital action for the self and also a vital action for the world. It is rather more important than hopping from a landing vehicle onto the moon's surface.

74. I can't say what this woman ought to do. I would understand it if she decided to take care of her mother and to not endanger herself. I would understand it if she decided to take a huge risk and demand that her siblings share in that onerous duty.

75. I would understand it if on Monday she felt one way, on Tuesday another way, and on Wednesday a third way. I would understand it if she felt strong resolve to buck the system, had a short chat with her aunt, and changed her mind completely.

76. I would understand it if she refused to take care of her mother. I would understand it if she felt too guilty and acquiesced. Who can say where a given individual will arrive? But let us hope that the decision she made was preceded by a step to one side.

77. We hold the intention to act ethically and to be good. That intention does nothing to eliminate moral complexities and ambiguities. Nor does it amount to a superpower able to defeat the forces of evil. But without that intention, where are we?

78. We hold that intention and then we act in human-sized ways. Sometimes that will mean nothing more than a kind word or a friendly gesture. Other times it will embroil us in

conflicts and make us enemies. At other times, it may mean revolution.

79. If goodness requires it, you may need to break a law. If goodness requires it, you may need to live dangerously. If goodness requires it, you may need to look the fool. If goodness requires it, you may need to shout. Ready or not.

80. Will you feel ready? Probably not. Nor may you feel very energetic. How can you put energy behind a choice about which you may still feel uncertain? But you must, finding or generating enough energy to honor the choice you've made.

81. You do this without any guarantee that you'll like the outcome. The consequences of an action, no matter how appropriate that action may be, aren't yours to control. You sigh, you act, and life plays itself out. We do not love this but we know this.

82. We say, "I do the next right thing." But we do not take that to mean, "I have perfect clarity" or "I feel assured." What it means is, "I'm trying." We try to act ethically and we try to do good. In a vortex of competing forces, we try to stay ethically upright.

83. Your neighbors may not join you in your decision to be good. That is terrible, but so be it. You know all about individuality, absurd rebellion, self-obligation, self-authorship, life purpose choosing, personal meaning-making, and our other kirist ideals.

84. Goodness must not be left out of the conversation. You grew up with pleasing cartoons that made everything simple. But you always knew better. Yes, it was lovely to root for this rabbit or to be schooled by that pig. Now we hold adult conversations.

85. We will always have to deal with self-interest. We will always be confronted by our safety and survival needs. We will always feel the shadows in our personality. That is, we are human. But we also know that we truly revere ethical action and goodness.

10

BOOK X. ORIGINAL PERSONALITY

1. Kirists think about personality. We are curious about who we are, how we form, why we think what we think, why we do what we do, and the extent to which human beings are the same as one another and different from one another.

2. Kirists grow aware that no textbook "theory of personality" feels very satisfying. Freud? Jung? Adler? Trait theory? There are dozens, but it's hard to find the person in personality theory. Who we know ourselves to be somehow isn't there.

3. So, we must come to our own understanding of personality. The tasks of self-obligation and self-authorship include coming to such a personal understanding. As we pursue that understanding, we see that new metaphors might be useful.

4. One useful metaphor is "original personality," a phrase that conjures ideas like "nature" and "temperament." Such

a phrase helps remind us about what human beings bring to the table at birth and what any given individual might bring.

5. A second useful metaphor is "formed personality." Kirists contrast original personality with formed personality. We suggest by the phrase "formed personality" the extent to which personality becomes rigid and fixed over time.

6. A third useful metaphor is "available personality." This phrase communicates the idea that while personality gets locked into place over time, severely reducing our ability to change, grow, and act freely, some amount of freedom still remains.

7. Thus, we conceptualize personality as comprised of three parts, original personality, formed personality, and available personality. A core kirist goal is to make use of our available personality to achieve the greater awareness of personhood.

8. "Personhood" is a fourth metaphor, as in "the movement from personality to personhood." Personhood is a state of better-than-average freedom from the bonds of personality and greater-than-average awareness to which kirists aspire.

9. None of this is more mysterious or harder to speak about than "original personality." How should we conceptualize that? How could that ever be investigated? How can we know anyone's original personality, including our own?

10. However, some things we can say. The first is obvious: that we are born already completely ourselves, in possession of some sort of "original personality." Every creature

is born already itself. Just look at puppies, kittens and infants.

11. One puppy really needs its mother while its brother is already off exploring. One kitten is sleepy all the time while its sister is a dynamo. One infant startles easily and her brother sleeps through anything. Creatures are fully themselves from birth.

12. Psychology pays no attention to this obvious truth because this truth is inconvenient. First, original personality is too hard to conceptualize. Second, it is impossible to investigate. Third, it undercuts the current "mental disorder" paradigm.

13. This avoidance makes the whole project of psychology a bit suspect. If you dub yourself "the science of human behavior" but take no interest in something that must be influential in determining that behavior, aren't you off on the wrong foot?

14. Psychology just skips it. But kirists mustn't. A kirist says, "Yes, I can't really distinguish between what is original to me and what I've become over time. But I do have my suspicions and some strong intuitions about my original nature."

15. Don't you have the sense that you were born somebody who, for instance, loved to sit in a corner reading a book? Who was skeptical of adult pronouncements? Who possessed a refined sense of justice and injustice? Doesn't all that feel familiar?

16. Or maybe it was some other set of qualities and attributes. Loving dresses, even though you were a boy. Obsessing about numbers. Being burdened by some

unnamable background sadness. Fearing spiders. Hearing music when others didn't.

17. However, even though we may feel that we know what sort of person we were at birth and sense who we were supposed to become, can we ever know if those feelings are accurate or more an artifact of our formed personality?

18. It is hard to see how we could know. Even if you asked some observer, say your wise uncle Max, what you were like as an infant and he replied that you were sensitive and shy, would that amount to a kind of an answer? Probably it wouldn't.

19. Probably we can't ever know. That makes original personality one of life's great mysteries. Occult systems like astrology exclaim, "No mystery there! As above, so below!" Kirists shake their head and reply, "I doubt that I can know for sure."

20. We likely can't know exactly who we were at birth, all of our suspicions, intuitions, and baby pictures notwithstanding. But despite that impenetrable mystery, we do know that original personality matters. Just knowing that gives us a huge leg up.

21. Without that awareness we might, for example, readily accept a label like "depression" for what we're feeling. With that awareness, we can sensibly ask: "What if I was born sad? Shouldn't we consider that a reasonable possibility?"

22. The fact that original personality is real, as real as genetics, carries with it all sorts of implications. First, there is the certainty that our original personality will prove challenging. It is bound to create pressure and make all sorts of demands.

23. If you're born with a ton of life energy, won't that amount to a demand? If you're born with a heightened sense of right and wrong, won't that amount to a demand? If you're born already craving alcohol, won't that amount to a demand?

24. In as many ways as we can conceive of original personality, in exactly that many ways may we find ourselves put upon by nature. Our particular nervous system, our particular brain, our particular consciousness: what a roster of demands!

25. Second, aspects of your original personality are bound to clash with aspects of your formed personality. Conflicts are inevitable. If, for instance, you've dumbed yourself down, won't your native intelligence get angry and snipe at you?

26. Picture all those conflicts. Not singing when a song is in your heart. Forcing yourself to stay still when every fiber demands motion. Struggling to hold your tongue when a lie is being promoted. Kirists know to expect violent clashes of this sort.

27. Third, aspects of your original personality are bound to make themselves felt all of a sudden, out of the blue. This will unsettle you, cause you to wonder what just happened, and maybe even make you doubt that you know yourself so well.

28. Say that a part of your original make-up is a heady egoism. Maybe you've done a yeoman's job of keeping that egoism under wraps. But one crisp autumn morning you burst out with some huge grandiosity. Isn't that day going to wobble?

29. Let's remind ourselves why "original personality" is so

very important to consider. It's vital because we've turned a blind eye to it and therefore have come to understand ourselves much more poorly than if we took its many realities into account.

30. Kirists, taking original personality into account, get ready for who we are and who we always will be. We are not surprised when some stray moonbeam brings on despair. We hate that, we wish that wouldn't happen, but we aren't surprised.

31. When, say, we get sad, we are slow to label that "the mental disorder of depression." Instead, we step to the side and ask ourselves, "Is sadness something I was built to experience? Let me consider that possibility before I pin on some label."

32. Or, say, we're pressured by our high energy levels and can't make ourselves sit still. We don't jump to call that "mania" or "attention deficit disorder." We say, "Wow, it looks like I was born with a ton of energy. How should I deal with that?"

33. Or, say, we find it hard to keep meaning afloat. We don't rail at ourselves for not finding "the meaning of life." Rather, we say, "As a smart, sensitive person, I can see right through to the void. I guess I was born to have problems with meaning."

34. We don't say, "I'm attracted to someone of the same sex. I must be sick." We don't say, "I have some powerful revenge fantasies. I must be sick." We don't say, "I don't like people very much. I must be a monster." We say, "How original!"

35. We can't know the exact contours of our original personality. But not forgetting the incontrovertible reality

of original personality changes everything. It is the equivalent of remembering, without embarrassment, that we are human.

36. Consider the important idea of readiness. Maybe we aren't "born sad," as if we were already frowning at birth. Maybe it is more that our original personality is such that we are ready to become sad, once we encounter the realities of the world.

37. Say that you were born bright, alert, and aware, with some inborn love of justice and some hatred of injustice. Doesn't that amount to a recipe for lifelong sadness? How can a bright, sensitive, ethical person not get regularly sad?

38. Even as a child you could distinguish between the stories that your parents were telling you and the reality you saw with your own two eyes. Your brand of consciousness saw this clearly and you found yourself shaking your head from birth.

39. You saw that one child was well-off because he was born into wealth and that another child was starving because he was born into poverty. You saw the reality behind the smile the clerk at the supermarket was forced to wear. You saw things.

40. These sights naturally made you sad. They made you sad for two reasons. First, it's dreadful that children starve to death and that clerks are forced to smile against their will. Second, it's dreadful that adults shut their eyes to these truths.

41. It wasn't that you had a genetic predisposition to something called "depression." To hunt for some gene or combination of genes would be the height of folly, as

would scanning your brain. No; by virtue of your very nature, sadness was coming.

42. To say that a person might be "born sad" isn't to say that he comes out of the womb frowning. Indeed, he may come out smiling. He may be a perfectly happy baby, a perfectly happy little human being who, however, is already on the brink.

43. He is primed for that sadness by virtue of his makeup. To put it the right way, he isn't "born sad," he is "born ready to be sad." And the world will meet him more than halfway. Given his nature and the nature of the world, sadness is coming.

44. He is "born ready to be sad" in the same sense that a shiny new car parked in Paris is "born ready to be dented." The reality is that no car's body or coat of paint can withstand the kind of banging bound to happen on Parisian side streets.

45. That shiny new car is "destined" to become a banged-up car because it is vulnerable to dents and because its situation is conducive to banging. It may be shiny when it leaves the factory but how will it look after a few years? Just a little sad?

46. Countless combinations of traits and attributes might lead to chronic sadness. Folks in that position weren't "born sad." They were born primed to be sad. Sadness was available to them and life, carelessly and indifferently, made it available.

47. Kirists remember not to automatically characterize some state as a disorder when it may be the playing out of "original personality meeting the world." There is no pill

to take when the issue is a beating heart slamming against a cruel world.

48. Consider the matter of consciousness itself. What if there are real differences between the consciousness of one person and the consciousness of another? Isn't that breathtaking to contemplate? What results might flow from such differences?

49. Consciousness in one person might create an experience of indwelling where everything was literal, where every teacup was exactly a teacup. Another person might be born with imagination, where teacups fly away at the slightest whim.

50. Is the first person, who, say, has become a banker, likely to be interested in the art of the second person, except, perhaps, as an investment? What if they are married to one another? Teacups all in a row and teacups flying this way and that?

51. What if human beings quite literally do not see the world in the same way? What if you see the hand of God where I see the natural world? What if you see numbers as magical and I see numbers as mathematics? How fundamental is that?

52. What if our original personality is some combustible mix of egoism and compassion, truthfulness and trickiness, a love of building and a love of destruction? Won't a combustible mix of that sort make us confused, upset, and unsettled?

53. Won't we feel like we hardly know ourselves? One minute we want to do the next right thing. The next minute we want to ruin everything, spoil someone's day,

spoil our own day, all for reasons we can't fathom—unless we remember it's in us.

54. Watch a child build his tower in all seriousness and then gleefully knock it down. More than one thing is going on in that child. Deep in his heart is a desire to make a wonderful thing. And deep in his heart is a desire to obliterate.

55. Maybe each of us is exactly such a combustible mix. Kirists presume that we are. We are not surprised that we might help our fellow creatures one moment and care nothing about them the next. We are honest and we expect that.

56. Our original nature isn't just one color, it is colorful. As Marsha, a study group participant put it, "I wasn't born one thing or another but rather completely available, available to love, to hate, to create, to destroy. And I'm still available."

57. Cynthia explained: "My formed personality is much politer than my original personality. I have a sarcastic streak that I keep hidden. The themes of humiliation and revenge that I play with in my head come from that original place."

58. From Nancy: "My original personality was innocent and very inquisitive. But I also had great anger. I think I needed the anger to deal with the world, which was no innocent place. I came into the world with both the innocence and the anger."

59. Whether or not these reports are strictly accurate, they speak to a truth. Human beings are not built with insides that are only pretty. Kirists do not run from that truth, as if

it were sinful. They say, "We are quite the creature! What a cocktail!"

60. They take that truth into account and do a much better job than average of accepting their urges, their idiosyncrasies, their out-of-left field impulses. They know that they want to help people get up—but maybe only after first tripping them.

61. The implications of original personality speak to a human reality more dynamic, more complicated, and maybe more interesting than the idea of a formed personality alone would suggest. Original personality produces amazing dynamism.

62. We are born; and along comes life. Our original personality is then hammered in the crucible of reality. Maybe we were born introverted; and then our home life feels so dangerous that we dive deeper inside, where we become melancholy.

63. That native introversion was original to us. That deeper, darker introversion was formed. Our already intense style of indwelling became airless and overheated. Life turned what might have been a lovely place of reflection into a prison cell.

64. Imagine if we began to ask the question, "What if a person is born primed to become sad and primed to become very sad if his experiences and his circumstances make matters worse?" Doesn't a question like that have great explanatory power?

65. We might even want to talk about a "primary" sadness that arises because we are built a certain way and a "secondary" sadness that arises because life piles on and

deepens our sadness. That way of speaking might prove very useful.

66. We might say, "I suspect that I was primed to become sad. Then my life experiences made me really sad. That doesn't translate into some pseudo-medical mental disorder. That is my exact nature dropped into my exact circumstances."

67. That way of thinking would help us distinguish between the secondary sadness arising because, say, we are currently unemployed, and the primary sadness that has dogged our heels for the longest time because we are built a certain way.

68. In that scenario, if you found an interesting job that might help ease your secondary sadness. But within days of getting that job, your "original sadness" might well return, making your new job suddenly feel altogether lackluster.

69. A kirist exclaims, "Caution! I may have been born with a susceptibility to chronic sadness, to chronic anxiety, to chronic obsessiveness, to chronic restlessness, to chronic boredom. I'd better be on guard and ready myself!"

70. Whether as a declaration or as a quiet conversation, you acknowledge your truth, for instance that boredom is bound to dog you. That boredom is an unwanted consequence of your original personality encountering the facts of existence.

71. You prepare yourself. You say, "I know what my life purposes are and I have a simple procedure, to do the next right thing. When some threat bubbles up from my original nature, I employ the super power of my life purposes to meet it."

72. You continue with, "I know that pesky sadness is right there, dogging my heels. But I have many important things to do, many self-obligations, and that's where I'm focusing. Maybe I can't kick sadness completely out the door but I can still live."

73. We are obliged to learn how to deal with the challenges that our original nature produces, challenges like an excess of life energy, background sadness, susceptibility to boredom, or whatever else it may be. This is a prime kirist self-obligation.

74. Most people do not take into account how endowments like intelligence, sensitivity, and rationality may together produce pathways to outcomes like chronic sadness. As a result, they end up surprised and confounded, rather than prepared.

75. Kirists prepare themselves. They acquire a working sense of the persistent challenges that their particular nature intends to throw at them. Then they step to one side, so as to apply awareness to what will prove a lifelong adventure in living.

76. Say that a powerful desire to withdraw into solitude wells up in you. But you know that you are needed on the front lines of a battle. You shake your head and say, "I know that I crave solitude. But my next right thing is to head to the front."

77. In this way, you honor your original personality without having to battle it or stand confused or confounded. You know that solitude is in your blood. But you also know what is required of you. You smile a little, nod, and pack your kit.

78. Organizing yourself around your life purposes isn't

likely to amount to a complete defense against the demands made by your original nature. But living such a purposeful way of life may prove a stout enough defense and must be worth a try.

79. Your nature will still make its urgent demands. It is a roiling thing comprised of everything that consciousness can throw up at you. It is at once readiness, blueprint, potentiality, and actuality. Yes, all that wildness is really there inside of you!

80. But you can get ready. And maybe even achieve something like peace. Can't you picture a day arriving when you hear yourself say, "Oh, hello there? Up to one of your tricks? How amusing! Mind if I just sip my tea and get on with things?"

81. We cross our fingers that we have sufficient awareness, freedom, available personality and wherewithal to deal with our original nature, whatever demands it makes, whatever it might whisper in our ear, whatever mayhem it might suggest.

82. At the same time, we laugh a little. How amazing that nature made a creature like us! Well, we must deal with what nature has wrought. We are not nearly as free as we need or want to be but we have a destiny to craft and a life to lead.

83. Original personality is powerfully influential but it is not our destiny. Our destiny must arise out of the molten interactions between our birth instructions and who we've become, all of that mediated by our ability to step to the side and be free.

84. If we are lucky and adamant, we make peace with our original personality, with its demands and its consequences.

And maybe we stand in awe, just as we stand in awe of an infant whose look tells us that she is coming from an ancient place.

85. Original personality is ancient information brought forth today in our particular package. We live with that nature, we make sense of it, and we adapt, striving to upgrade the cacophony of personality into the quiet pride of personhood.

11

BOOK XI. PSYCHOLOGICAL ENTANGLEMENTS

1. A contemporary philosophy of life must be psychological. Kirism asserts that what was previously treated as purely philosophical, religious, or spiritual must now be moved to the realm of the strictly human, where psychology dominates.

2. A philosophy of life isn't about the lives of bees or roses. It is about how members of a particular species are built, interact, and might want to live. Maybe we are obliged to call it a philosophy of human life, just to be as clear as possible.

3. Previously philosophies and religions only rarely mirrored observed human life. Rather, they were tales spun to support agendas. Sometimes they were fairy tales. Sometimes they were teaching tales. That is, they were works of fiction.

4. Science, too, created its works of fiction. It made believe that by looking at a brain scan you would know whether someone despaired or loved cribbage. It made believe that

science could explain why someone preferred poetry to prose.

5. Kirism rejects that psychiatry, Taoism, Marxism, Hinduism, the social sciences, Judaism, socialism, Islam, Christianity, and even psychology itself is psychological enough or even very psychological at all. Do we see real people there? Or just incense and agendas?

6. Kirism asserts that science, social science, philosophy, and religion haven't taken into sufficient account—or, too often, any account—the psychological realities of human beings. They have managed countless words while leaving people out.

7. Therefore, those systems stand mute and helpless, or frothy with platitudes, in the face of the events of real life, like this girl with everything to live for committing suicide or that nation turning far to the right when yesterday it looked progressive.

8. Some traditions, still followed by billions, make the claim that all you need to know about life purpose can be found in a certain book—the old Testament, the new Testament, the Koran. A God is posited; you are to bow; His will be done.

9. Kirists reply, "I may be a product, but I am not that sort of product. I am a complicated psychological creature, not a favored or ill-favored child of mystical parents. My life purposes are not provided, they are the chosen fruits of my own wisdom.

10. Then kirists smile. As students of psychological reality, they understand how limited that wisdom may be, how their selfish genes may be influencing their life purposes,

how their formed personality may be making a mockery of the idea of freedom.

11. Still, they try to make some sense of real life. Kirism is an aspirational philosophy, asking human beings to do the right thing, and it is also an investigative philosophy, asking human beings to study how the mind works and how human beings operate.

12. Kirists look to the person, not to outer space. We look to the couple fighting, not to spirits in the woods. We look to the family bully assaulting his children, not to pathways to nirvana. We look at people: at how they are the same and how they are different.

13. We look at this exact life, full of love and envy and hatred and productivity and sloth and mobs and compassion and all the rest; and not at past lives, at make-believe lives, at the lives of the saints, at the sayings of gurus, or at anything else distracting.

14. In the process, we arrive at our ways of conceptualizing human life. We consider the ideas of original personality, formed personality, and available personality. We think about the tension between our humanistic impulses and our selfish genes.

15. We consider it all, we make up our own language if new words and phrases are needed, we rethink ideas like "ego" and "the unconscious." We stand directly in front of consciousness and inquire about it. We travel inside and look at how the mind operates.

16. As we investigate, we are bound to arrive at the idea of psychological entanglements. We discern that we experience life as a spider's web of entanglements. Life is sticky,

knotted, and unfree-feeling. Everywhere we turn is another knot.

17. The textbook definition of psychology is as follows: "Psychology is the science of behavior." Ha! Psychology ought to be conceptualized as the investigation of psychological entanglements. It should be the study of knots.

18. Your father is a real person but he is also a psychological entanglement. You are still tangled up with the way you read disappointment in his glance thirty years ago as you practiced the piano. Something is still stuck there, knotted and tangled.

19. How entangled? I posted a piece to my *Psychology Today* blog titled, "I hate my mother." It got 400,000 views. I received daily emails from readers: "That's me!" How many people, kirists among them, are tangled up in the lifelong hatred of someone?

20. You go to war. You have terrible experiences. You come home troubled. Kirists don't say, "You have an illness." We don't say, "You have PTSD." We say, you are all tangled up, caught like a fish on a hook, unable to leave those horrors and that guilt behind.

21. What is an obsessive thought? An entanglement. It isn't as if the thought is like pleasant background music. No! That isn't how an obsessive thought is experienced. It's experienced as a thing with claws. It's got its tentacles into you!

22. What is despair? Another entanglement. The sadness is a heavy overcoat, a straightjacket, chains. Streamers of flypaper hang everywhere: when you try to move, you get stuck. This happens too often and you stop caring about moving—or about anything.

23. Language entangles. You happen upon the phrase "archaeological dig." You spin out a fantasy. How splendid that dig would be! You don't think "hot sun, aching back, slim rewards." No! You think, "Amazing!" And so, you have created an entanglement.

24. Self-image is an entanglement. Maybe you are all tangled up with the need to look good, even perfect. You do something that reflects poorly on you. Too tangled up to tell the truth, you blame the weather, the wind, and how the sun got in your eyes.

25. Imagine if we had permission to be ourselves, warts and all, and didn't get tangled up in caring how we look? But we do get tangled up like that, so much so that nations go to war just because their leaders are preening and protecting their self-image.

26. Identity is another entanglement. You are born into a Baptist family. And so, you identify with everything Baptist and get tangled up with everything Baptist. There is no separation between you and that. Every verse of scripture is an entanglement!

27. Worse, we possess multiple identities, each of which entangles. Woman. Muslim. Pakistani. Upper class. Devoted daughter. Wife-who-must-produce-babies. Less favored younger sister. We are ten things, twenty things, and all are entangling.

28. Almost anything can entangle. An instantaneous glimpse of something and we are entangled with that something for life. Maybe it's the look of a night café. Maybe it's the look on our mother's face. It's as if certain experiences come with the strongest glue!

29. Why should that be? What can be the evolutionary bene-

fits of such painful entanglements, such intense, almost unbreakable connections that rival the universe's strong force in their ability to get their hooks into us? What is nature up to?

30. Maybe nature is clever and wise. Because, why would we do anything unless something got its hooks into us? Isn't behavior exactly the playing out of entanglements? Don't we do what we do because something has gotten its hooks into our flesh?

31. Maybe nature has concocted this precise way of motivating us. Maybe it's played another one its little tricks and can't help but laugh: "Freedom? Right! I need you to do exactly what I say. So, I shall entangle you in the most devious ways!"

32. And so, nature entangles us up with, say, our mean-spirited family. It forces us to show up at Thanksgiving dinner not for the turkey, not for the biscuits, not for the scintillating conversation, but for the sake of the species.

33. We go despite knowing that uncle Jack will annoy us and that aunt Margaret will subtly insult us. We go despite knowing that we will put on three pounds. We go despite knowing that we will regret going. We go because we are hooked and can't not go.

34. Or, say, we attend cattle call auditions for small parts where a hundred other actors are also auditioning because we're tangled up in the idea of our acting career. Some voice is commanding, "You must do this, even if it is demeaning and ridiculous."

35. Maybe all behavior flows from entanglements. Maybe all motivation does, too. Certainly, much of it must. Isn't sexual attraction an entanglement? Aren't you drawn to

that gorgeous person as if a hook had been attached to your collar?

36. Aren't you pulled closer and closer? Is that magnetism? Or is it dangerous entanglement? Now you are right in that person's space, whether or not it is wise to be there, whether or not being that close is really the next right thing to be doing.

37. Nature creates a creature who must stay motivated in order to stay alive. Without motivation, we would stay in bed and starve to death. How to keep us motivated? Build in hooks. Hook us so fiercely that we have hardly any say in the matter.

38. If this is what nature has done, then we must be careful. To rid ourselves of entanglements might be to accidentally rid ourselves of motivation. Perfect disentanglement might mean zero energy, zero passion, zero curiosity, zero motivation.

39. Isn't a lot of Buddhist depression exactly that: the mindful shedding of entanglements, followed by detachment, followed by a lack of motivation, followed by chronic sadness? You are gloriously detached; but what is life really like without any hooks at all?

40. We begin to see the outline of two kirist goals. One is to carefully disentangle. We want the freedom to skip that Thanksgiving dinner, to skip a career just because a bit of language seduced us, to not have affairs when we shouldn't.

41. A second goal is to find the way to remain motivated while living life as unentangled as possible. This is a beautiful idea and connects to other kirist ideas: that we can

coax meaning into existence, that we can live our life purposes.

42. Another way to conceptualize these twin goals is that we can simultaneously attach and detach. We can invest in life: that is attachment. We can also unhook where we do not want to invest. That is detachment. Those are a pair of wonderful high-bar goals!

43. If we can do this, we are also practicing energy wisdom. We want energy bubbling up: then we have fuel for living. But we don't want our energy tenaciously hooked onto a worry, a regret, or a bad idea. We want our life energy to flow freely.

44. If we can do this, we are honoring our obligation to awareness. We are saying, "I agree to pay attention to where I am hooked. I get it. I am a psychological creature liable to get shackled to a custom, a memory, a person, to almost anything."

45. Awareness disentangles. That crucial kirist step to the side, that sidestep that gives us the chance to think, to judge, to figure out what's going on and what the next right thing ought to be, spares us so much folly!

46. But that sidestep can hurt. What happens when you try to untangle your knotted hair? It hurts. What happens when you try to step to the side of an entanglement, so as to get a better view of it? That can hurt tremendously.

47. You try to step to the side of your marriage, to see it for what it is. But pain courses through as you try, the pain of failure, of regret, of embarrassment. You can hardly manage that sidestep, so much pain is your effort generating.

48. You try to step to the side of your career. You know that your career isn't what you'd hoped it would be. You know that it must be examined. But you are pierced by pain as you try to move, hooked onto the hope you still have for your lifelong love.

49. You try to step to the side of your creative project, that narrative painting that is boring you. As you try, you discover that you are still painfully hooked to the painting's subject matter, that story you are hoping to tell about good and evil.

50. Part of you understands that the painting is a cliché. Part of you understands that it can't be rendered well enough with your actual skill set. Part of you understands that you are engaged in folly. But the idea remains painfully hooked in your brain.

51. You try to step to the side of your belief system, to see if you still believe what you think you believe. But you can hardly budge. Is glue the right image? Flypaper? A hook? Whatever the right image, the effort required is almost super-human.

52. Tolerating the inevitable pain that we will experience when we try to remove a powerful hook is a kirist self-obligation. As with so many other things in life, kirists do not suppose that this will be easy and do not need it to be easy.

53. We try at least not to be surprised by the pain. We accept that psychological entanglements are like thorn bushes and we invite the pain of untangling. We tolerate it, for the sake of our freedom and for the sake of right living.

54. We may also come to realize that there is a certain painless change that we can make. We see that we can

begin to change the grammar of our existence. We can revise our language constructions to better serve the goal of disentanglement.

55. Imagine saying, "I am tangled up with sadness" instead of "I am sad." Can you feel the really useful work that linguistic change would make? Suddenly you have a perspective on what you're feeling and a better understanding of what you're feeling.

56. You might then nod and murmur, "Oh. It isn't that I am this thing called 'sad.' It's that I'm being made sad by the way my mind entangles me. If I could free myself of these entanglements, I might not be 'sad' at all. How interesting."

57. You might begin to wonder, "Is sadness the problem or is it the entanglements?" This very wonder opens the window and lets a breeze in. Your next thought might be, "Maybe I'm not sad at all! Maybe I just need to get some hooks released!"

58. This simple linguistic tactic, of substituting "I'm tangled up with X" for "I'm X," can do a brilliant job of helping explain you to you and a brilliant job of actually effecting change. Those few additional words might make a huge difference.

59. Imagine saying "I am tangled up with my hatred of my mother" instead of "I hate my mother." Suddenly you may not feel hatred at all. Something might have gotten loosened, lightened, unknotted. A deep sigh might follow.

60. Imagine saying, "I am tangled up with my need for this career," instead of "My career is going nowhere." Rather than sinking into sadness, you might feel motivated to get

unentangled. Your next steps might suddenly become clear to you.

61. You can begin to build in an awareness of the reality of entanglements, and better comprehend the nature of your particular entanglements, simply by reminding yourself in this simple way, by creating this new linguistic habit.

62. Another painless change and alteration to the grammar of our existence that kirists can make is to murmur, “How strange and subtle” when we witness our entanglements in action. We notice, shake our head, and whisper, “How precisely human of me.”

63. As a child, you pass by a women’s house of detention twice a day, as you go to school and as you come home again. You watch the women at the windows. Thirty years later, you’ve become a photographer, chronicling the lives of incarcerated women.

64. How strange and subtle. Who knew that passing that prison would amount to a lifelong hook? Why that prison and not the fire station you passed each day, or that grand old hotel, or that old mill? How strange and subtle. Makes one almost smile.

65. As a child, you began to feel certain that your parents were not your biological parents. You started what would become lifelong investigations, inquiring of great aunts, sneaking looks in old document boxes, examining the faces of strangers.

66. One day you manage to shake your head and murmur, “How strange and subtle.” You stand there amazed. “How strange that I became obsessed with this, and at what a cost! I’ve put my life on hold over this. Now I’m done with it!”

67. These tenacious psychological entanglements aren't just casual mental connections or mildly contributory causes. They are thieves that can steal a whole life. Maybe, say, the hook is beauty—and with that hook comes a lifetime of cosmetic surgery.

68. Maybe the hook is body image and a lifetime of starvation and self-disgust. Maybe the hook is masculinity and a lifetime of macho antics. Maybe the hook is the idea of genius and a lifetime of disappointment at your "intellectual shortcomings."

69. If these were mere connections, you could disconnect. If these were mere causes, you could add new links to that chain of cause-and-effect and manage a desired change. But it isn't like that, is it? Psychological entanglements get their fangs into you.

70. I've been tangled up with Judaism my whole life, just as born Catholics get tangled up with Catholicism or born Muslims get tangled up with Islam. How could a person born into a religion, into a set of customs and rules, and into a community not get entangled there?

71. That entanglement might become a lifelong affectionate relationship, leading a girl to dream of becoming a nun and motivating her to still dream of vows late in life. In fact, she may have taken a powerful vow—say, a vow of poverty—without even knowing it.

72. Or it might become a lifelong antagonistic relationship, with the very look of Hasidim breeding raw fury in an atheistic Jew. That hook can have you shaking your head out of the blue, for no reason that you can name, just because you happened to pass a synagogue.

73. Affectionate or antagonistic, it is a hook. You may

unnecessarily love something because of such a hook. You may unnecessarily hate something because of such a hook. Either way, you are being robbed and misdirected.

74. Say that you are thinking a useful thought, maybe about a plot point in your novel. A small thing happens—you catch your reflection in a shop window—and it connects to one of your hooks, about body image. Goodbye novel!

75. Hooks do precisely that sort of everyday damage. And they limit your possibilities. Aren't you going to stand indifferent to things you might otherwise appreciate, because you are hooked in so many other places? Hooks prevent chances.

76. Kirists pay attention to these ideas. They examine their antics and their motivations and they wonder, "Is this my best self in action or is this some hook playing itself out?" They add these ideas to their other ideas about human nature and personality.

77. But, can you really know all of your reasons for any of your behaviors: your complete set of reasons, say, for painting abstractly? How many of those reasons may be "right" and how many "wrong"? And if they are an inexplicable mix of the two, what then?

78. What then? Well, you take your step to the side and you try your best to understand. There is nothing else for a human being to do. But, by knowing about hooks and by looking for hooks, you at least give yourself a decent chance of comprehending.

79. And maybe you actually figure something out. Maybe you escape a lifelong trap. Congratulations! How brilliant of you! How dexterous! So, you stride off, your chest

puffed out—and encounter more flypaper. The flypaper is everywhere!

80. Life isn't just one psychological entanglement. Life isn't just two psychological entanglements. Life is a web and a network of them. We disentangle here and get re-entangled or newly entangled there. Life is sticky like that.

81. Experiences are sticky like that. The cruelties of your authoritarian parents are rightly called traumatic. Those traumas infiltrated you and helped create your formed personality. Now we have another way of thinking about what is still going on: you remain entangled.

82. Really, isn't that what we mean by trauma? Something happened to us and we are not over it, not by a longshot. It is still with us. How? As psychological entanglements that play themselves out as every manner of disturbance and difficulty.

83. Kirists assert that it is better to think in terms of the entangling nature of experience than to pejoratively label people as neurotic, personality disordered, obsessive-compulsive or narcissistic. Don't those labels just create more entanglements?

84. The idea of psychological entanglement is not the complete word on human psychology. But it is a useful, true-to-life construct with a lot of explanatory power. It is a go-to question to ask as we try to navigate life: "Am I hooked here? Am I entangled? Am I in some grip?"

85. Human beings are indeed "in the grip." Kirists understand this, about themselves and about everyone. This makes the notion of human freedom rather dubious. At the same time, kirists affirm: "We get it. Still, we can be freer. That is our work."

12

BOOK XII. WORK

1. Philosophies of life rarely concern themselves with something as mundane as the work that we do. But work is a huge affair in the lives of actual human beings. It takes up our time, it wears us out, it inhabits our mind, and it partially defines who we are.

2. What, for example, if the work that you do has no connection to your life purpose choices except that it meets the basic life purpose need of sheer survival? Aren't you going to resent that work a lot and continually dream about doing something else?

3. Or, to take a different sort of example, say that you are doing work that holds meaning for you but the actual doing of it is an unpleasant experience. You desperately want to write a novel but the writing of it is torture. How difficult will that prove?

4. Or, as a third example, say that you are a stay-at-home parent raising children and running a household. Even though you work every moment of the day, will it feel like

you have "real work"? And will the world credit you with doing "real work"?

5. A recent poll put the number of workers who hate their jobs at 85%. Other polls have put the number at "only" 70%. Are all of these workers malcontents? Or is work the problem? It looks like we have another epidemic, but what is the actual problem?

6. Work is indeed the problem. It is hard to tolerate even the work that we ourselves dream up. Kirists know that it has always been like this. They know that work is no innocuous, incidental, or smiley-faced thing. It is something else; and often brutal.

7. Work is something that steals away one-third or one-half of our life. It may pay the rent but it is also a thief. For some people, a lucky few, this is not the case. For most people, it is. For most people, work is a burden, an albatross, and even a killer.

8. Why should the work that most people do not suit their human needs? Let's try to picture ideal work, work that fits us so well and pleases us so well that we don't even think of it as work. What would work of that sort look like and feel like?

9. Ideal work would provoke the psychological experience of meaning. It would feel interesting. It would match our moral calculus. It would match our personality and identity. It would pay well enough. And it would not exhaust or overwhelm us.

10. It would also come with certain bonuses and benefits, like, for instance, a sense of community. These extras might actually matter a lot. Maybe we need our work to

provide us with a sense of prestige. Maybe we need it to make us feel powerful.

11. Maybe we crave a rock-and-roll lifestyle and need our work to provide it. Maybe we crave respectability and need that from our work. Maybe we need our work to allow us to be our most creative self. We may need our work to do all of this and more.

12. Can any work match this ideal? A teacher may love her work but not be paid decently. A lawyer may love what she does, except for the ethics of it. A social worker may find her work valuable but burn out doing it. A poet may never earn a cent.

13. Let's say that we did find ideal work. Then we would need the world not to change, the work not to change, and we ourselves not to change. How likely is that? How likely is it that a Starbucks wouldn't open up right across from our sweet café?

14. Imagine the difference between delivering the mail when the mail consisted of letters from sweethearts, grandchildren and faraway friends, rather than what it now consists of, tons and tons of unwanted supermarket ads. Is such a change tolerable?

15. What are the odds of competitors never appearing? What are the odds of your work interesting you forever? What are the odds of cultural cataclysms not changing everything? What are the odds of you not being transferred or remaindered?

16. So, for work to feel tolerable, we need it to meet a great many criteria, too many really, and at the same time we need nothing to change, no new boss, no new technology,

no creeping boredom. Where did we get the idea this could be possible?

17. After I got out of the Army and graduated from college, I briefly worked for the Veterans Administration as a veterans' benefits counselor. Veterans would come into the office with their concerns and questions and we counselors tried to help them.

18. I saw one veteran after another. In my naiveté, I thought the idea was to help each veteran expeditiously and to get right on to the next needy veteran. I did this for about a day-and-a-half before I was summoned into my supervisor's office.

19. He explained to me that I was seeing too many veterans and making everyone else look bad. I had to slow down. I had to slow down a lot. His message was perfectly clear. I would not survive my probationary period if I kept working this fast.

20. That didn't sit so well with me. Soon I left. Next, I talked my way into a job as a proofreader at the American Meteorological Society. I had never previously done any proofreading but I crammed, learned a few symbols, passed a test, and got hired.

21. The challenge with this job was that it was stupendously mind-numbing. It wasn't just dealing with paragraph after paragraph of jargon-drenched minutia. It was also that, as a double-check, we were to read each line backwards, to catch any last errors.

22. Backwards! Yes, you might indeed discover that a "the" had been spelled "teh." But what sort of salary would it take to sit there, straining your eyes and your nerves for

forty hours a week, scanning lines backwards? More than they were paying.

23. Then I got an odd job "judging contests." I'd travel around the country to radio stations and "officially" select the winner of the contest that the station was running. The prize was typically some up-and-coming band appearing at a local high school.

24. I'd cover my eyes and pluck a name out of a bowl. I'd show the deejay the putative "winning" entry and as often as not he'd shut our mikes and whisper something like, "It can't be a junior high school kid. Pick again!"

25. So, I would pick again. And maybe pick again, until we got to the "perfect" winner. I'm sure that repeated picking wasn't the worst sin the world has ever seen. You and I could both name graver ones. But I couldn't do that job for very long, either.

26. Then I sold encyclopedias door-to-door. I memorized the pitch and went out with my trainer. It was instantly clear to me that the poor folks I was pestering shouldn't buy the overpriced encyclopedia set I was hawking. One evening and done.

27. Then, through some fortunate connections, I got a writer's dream job. I started ghostwriting. I loved writing and I loved being paid for writing. Indeed, it met a great many of the criteria for ideal work. Except, unfortunately, the ethical.

28. First, someone else's name would appear on each of these books for hire. Did it matter that readers thought they were getting a book written by Joe or Jane? That probably wasn't a giant fraud. But weren't readers being duped just a little?

29. Then, was it really proper to, for example, write a book about "the best singles' bars in America" without visiting any? (I used Chamber of Commerce handouts.) Well, who was I hurting by sending folks to some well-liked fern bar in Houston? But still.

30. More tellingly, was it okay to write an arthritis guide when I knew nothing about arthritis? This well-paid one I just couldn't make myself do. Instead, I handed it off to a friend, who tackled it gleefully, creating a book's worth of made-up arthritis cures.

31. Then there was the book about biorhythms. I was asked to confer the mantle of research on some very dubious ideas about human rhythms promulgated by Wilhelm Fliess, an eye-ear-nose-and-throat doctor and Freud's cocaine connection.

32. I did the research, wrote the book, debunked Fliess, and said some sensible things about biorhythms. The book appeared, carrying the name of a well-known clinical psychologist and turning around everything that I had said about Fliess.

33. Well, that was it for ghostwriting. It was perfect work but dubious. I mourned the loss of that wonderful writer's gig, one that was allowing me to write my novels, and faced once again the need to acquire that ravenous eater of life and time, a job.

34. I went into training to become a psychotherapist. I found it curious that after not so many classes, very few of which prepared us to do anything in particular, we were supposed to be able to "diagnose and treat mental disorders." Amazing!

35. It was clear that my peers loved calling the folks they

saw "patients," as if they were surgeons. I knew that something fishy was afoot and I've spent the last thirty years writing about the serious shortcomings of psychiatry and psychotherapy.

36. I could go on. If I asked you, you could go on. It isn't just that work is "hard." It's that so much of work doesn't sit well. It is so solidly embedded in a world of tedium, bottom lines, difficult personalities, dubious ethics and contentious mini-dramas.

37. And work takes up so much time! Maybe we could survive terrible work that lasted just an hour a day. But eight full hours! Add in those lost hours before and after, commuting or brooding about the job. Should half a life be spent this way?

38. Given that work is exactly like this, what ought a kirist to do? Are there some better plans, better strategies, better options? Is there any way to move work from the albatross side of the ledger to the status of acceptable or even satisfying?

39. Unless we are independently wealthy or otherwise supported and provided for, we need to make money in order to survive. Kirists, like everyone, must factor in the matter of livelihood when they try to strategize handling the challenges of work.

40. And human beings need to feel occupied. In a core existential sense, we can't not work. Yes, we can take vacations. Yes, we can spend stretches of time at sea, in transition, or otherwise not quite occupied. But for the most part, we need occupation.

41. Occupation and livelihood are bedrock needs. Then, we have our many wants: that the work interest us, that the

work feels moral to us, that the work provides us with certain perks, like a sense of community, a chance to be creative, and so on.

42. Given these core needs and these many wants, how shall we approach work? Consider someone who is currently engaged in what he considers to be meaningless work and who is also learning about kirism. How might he approach the matter?

43. Consider Harry, who finds his corporate job both taxing and meaningless. When a person says, "My job is meaningless," we don't imagine that spending a month on an ashram will do much to change his experience of work when he returns to it.

44. That month away may help him see that he ought to quit his job. It may help him talk himself into feeling more positive about his job. It may have some other useful consequences. But work will again begin to eat him alive the moment he returns to it.

45. The long and the short of it is that Harry hates his job. He's certain he's obliged to do something that he's characterizing as "something radical." But what exactly? He takes his kirist learning to heart and decides to do all of the following.

46. First, he creates his list of life purposes. He finds this task grueling but, as luck would have it, an item on the list sparks his interest. His diabetic sister living in South America has always had trouble procuring her insulin. This gets him thinking.

47. Next, he mulls over the matter of individuality. He considers his need for it, the challenges associated with it, and who he might want to be from now on in. He hears

himself say, "I need to be the individual that I really am." This gets him thinking.

48. Next, he takes to heart the idea of absurd rebellion. Harry is aware that he has been a "go along to get along" person. The idea of rebellion ties his stomach in knots. But he finds himself nodding to himself: is it time to take some necessary risks?

49. He thinks about the phrase "from personality to personhood." In considering it, he senses how his formed personality has aimed him at safe, reliable work that he detests. Can he now make use of his remaining freedom to achieve personhood?

50. He begins to take to heart the kirist demand that what he does be moral, worthy, and aligned with the multiple meanings of the phrase "Do the next right thing." His current job is morally neutral at best. His next work really must be higher-minded.

51. He enters the "room that is his mind" and takes notice of his indwelling style. He makes a mental note of some needed improvements, like adding windows and installing a safety valve to reduce the constant pressure he feels.

52. He comes to realize that he has not been authoring his own life. Maybe he's been doing a decent job of accepting his lot. But a life of headaches and stomachaches from attending boring meetings about sales projections really must stop.

53. First, he makes a decision. He will start his own business. He does some research and discovers that no one is devoted to providing low-cost insulin internationally. Of course, this may prove fantastically hard to do. But he embraces the challenge.

54. He starts his day earlier, and with a new orientation. His orientation is no longer toward his miserable work day. Now when he wakes up he spends a full hour on his new business. Sometimes he spends two hours, even if that makes him late.

55. Building his business is even harder than he imagined it would be. And, so far, it feels less meaningful than he had hoped it would feel. But he knows to align his thoughts with his intentions and to repeat to himself, "I'm building my business."

56. He attends to the needs of his budding business for that hour with as little drama as possible. He doesn't always love that hour but he knows that it is the exact right thing for him to be doing from five a.m. to six a.m. each day.

57. At work, he manifests his chosen personality upgrades. He practices calmness and detachment, he reminds himself not to evaluate life negatively just because he is obliged to work, and he regulates his energy, avoiding gearing up into speediness.

58. At lunch, which he now takes every day, he invests meaning in "just being" and goes for a walk to a certain park a quarter mile from his office, where he eats his sandwich. He uses this time to breathe and to relax; and he doesn't rush himself back.

59. In the afternoon, he gets his salaried work done and at the same time makes use of his breaks to do some work on the insulin business, sending out an email, writing website copy, or seeing how nonprofits similar to his have designed themselves.

60. When he leaves work, he really leaves it behind him. Rather than joining colleagues and stopping for a few too

many drinks, he leisurely strolls to a bus stop a full mile away, enjoying the afternoon bustle, the city sights, and the light of dusk.

61. When he gets home, he takes a shower and then makes a mindful choice as to whether he will relax by watching a few episodes of the television show he is currently following or whether he will invest an hour in his insulin business.

62. Was that a splendid day or a perfect day? Perhaps not. But it was certainly an intentional day and a better day than those that he'd been experiencing before deciding to organize his life around his life purposes. It was a day to make Harry proud.

63. Some evenings, Harry attends to another of his newly-identified life purpose choices: relationships. Harry has come to realize that he has always been too much of a loner, a bit too shy, a bit too alienated, a bit too disinterested. Now he works on that.

64. Employing a dating site, Harry meets Mary, a teacher. They go out two nights a week and talk often. Something lovely is blooming between them and effortlessly, without them having to say much about it, they begin seeing each other exclusively.

65. Harry is making use of his available personality to reclaim himself. He has consciously reduced his defensiveness so as to begin dating and he continues to work on maintaining a positive evaluation of life, even as his day job drags him down.

66. Let's follow Harry for a little longer. It turns out that he and Mary fall in love, which makes his life lighter and lovelier. It also turns out that she enjoys her job and makes

enough for the two of them to live on. This allows Harry to think about quitting.

67. He doesn't yet quit, but he does further distance himself from his day job. At the same time, he squeezes in more hours on his insulin business. That business, which he started with modest aims, keeps growing in his mind, in his heart, and in actuality.

68. The phrase "Do the next right thing" continues to resonate. Harry thinks about what might help people live slightly less hard lives, begins to do things that help people live slightly less hard lives, and gets real satisfaction from doing these things.

69. Not only does he feel pride in his choices, he experiences meaning from his choices. Life feels much more meaningful now that he has the insulin business to invest in and Mary in his life. Indeed, he doesn't "think about meaning" much at all.

70. With real trepidation, because it scares him not to receive a paycheck and because it scares him to rely on himself, Harry quits his corporate job. Life doesn't suddenly become carefree or easy but he is wise enough not to expect such outcomes.

71. Harry is of course still a human being. He has his sour days and his misadventures. Sometimes he can't help brooding about world events; sometimes he can't help brooding about his weight; sometimes he can't help brooding about his demise.

72. But his life is altogether better. Work that matters and a loving relationship have changed everything. He rarely pines for meaning; he rarely pines for life to be different.

Maybe with just a hint of irony in the gesture, he gives life a thumb's up.

73. Harry can now make use of his abundant energy in ways that serve him, that serve others, and that feel meaningful to him. He wears a smile of satisfaction even as he deals with the red tape that comes with trying to distribute insulin across borders.

74. Harry's saga underscores why so many kirists find themselves becoming solo entrepreneurs. By creating their own work, they better meet their self-obligations and more fully engage in self-authorship. There's a kirist logic to solo entrepreneurship.

75. There are reasons why so many people today are attempting some version of the one-person business. That possibility exists in ways that never existed before the Internet. Kirism, as a contemporary philosophy, factors in this new, exciting reality.

76. Having to work at something isn't the issue, since human beings need to feel occupied, invested, tested, and alive. Our life purpose needs aren't met by the complete absence of work. The issue is how occupations play themselves out in reality.

77. Kirists understand that every line of work is likely to prove challenging. Even the cushioned, protected life of the college professor may come with boredom, disinterested undergrads, failed lines of research, and the dramas of department politics.

78. Other-created work is taxing. Self-created work is taxing. Harry may be thrilled to leave his corporate job behind but does anyone imagine that his insulin business

won't come with a really staggering number of challenges and disappointments?

79. We step to one side and examine work as clearly and as calmly as we can. Do I want to live as a writer? As a yoga teacher? As a life coach? As a lawyer? As a baker? As a painter? Well, what exactly does that entail, today and not in some bygone time?

80. We make our choices and then we learn the truth about our choices by living. We start a business and discover what running a business means. We become a teacher and learn what teaching means. We do the work and then understand.

81. How could it be otherwise? Maybe when you were a child you watched your father run his general store. How much can that teach you about running a store in the cyber age? You will have to try out your contemporary version and learn by trying.

82. Children are asked "What do you want to be?", as if they were choosing candy from a candy store. Oh, look at all these lovely professions! Firefighter or astronaut! Ski instructor or brain surgeon! Work is romanticized right from the beginning.

83. Or maybe it's presented in the opposite way, as your human lot, as necessary drudgery, as something that pays the bills, as something not to question, as something to be thankful for. It may be presented as a heavy load all human beings must lug.

84. Either way, we aren't adequately educated about the nature of work and the realities of work. So, we must learn the truth about work for ourselves. Any sensible philosophy

of life should underscore the need for this grown-up understanding.

85. A living philosophy acknowledges every difficult human reality. Kirists say, "We are obliged to occupy ourselves and we know just how hard work can be." Then they roll up their sleeves and strive to find or invent the work that will serve them best.

13

BOOK XIII. ENERGY WISDOM

1. It takes so much energy to live a kirist life. All those life purposes! All those daily practices! All that doing the next right thing and the right thing after that! All that saving the world! So much energy is required to live a kirist life.

2. Ah, but it takes energy to live *any* life. Living requires energy. Without energy, human beings sink to their knees or take to their beds. No food for weeks? No reasons to live? No respite from stress? No break from overwhelm? Then, exhaustion.

3. Life requires energy and living generates energy and also steals energy. A sudden passion and we are full of energy. A sudden defeat and the energy drains right out of us. This is nothing like the simple mechanics of a toy stopping when its battery dies.

4. Human energy is no simple affair. Say that you crave more passion in your life. You decide to throw yourself into a creative project. Your energy soars! But then you have

trouble sleeping or relaxing. Was turning yourself on really such a good idea?

5. Well, you wanted the passion. But not all those consequences! Imagine racing down the road with the top down and the wind whipping your hair. Lovely! But what if you are going too fast to negotiate that bend in the road? There you go, flying off a cliff!

6. Energy! We must get wiser about human energy. We need to understand what steals it, what creates it, when it is safe to increase it, what to do if our blood is boiling, and what to do if our energy has vanished: all its peculiarities and subtleties.

7. Energy! It should be a subject taught in schools. There should be energy experts the equivalent of electrical engineers. Experts who can talk smartly about passion, listlessness, apathy, obsession, concentration, mania, distraction ...

8. Nothing is more fundamental to human life than energy. But we have few good ways of speaking about energy. When it comes to machines, we can talk about joules, watts and amperes. But when it comes to humans, we stand tongue-tied.

9. This lack of energy language prevents us from taking a fundamental feature of human existence into account. Imagine chatting about the relationships among celestial objects without a notion of gravity. What nonsense would ensue!

10. Indeed, we are rather talking nonsense when we fail to credit the extent to which states like passion, obsession, compulsion, and mania, on the one hand, and boredom,

listlessness, mental fatigue and despair, on the other hand, are energy states.

11. We don't even know if we are for energy or against it! When we say that a child has high energy, aren't we practically indicting him? We claim that his antics amount to a "mental disorder." His high energy is at best a terrible inconvenience.

12. Wouldn't parents snap up a device to drain away all that energy? Oh, but what would you have then? A lethargic child. Now you have "pediatric depression." Now a device to infuse him with energy! And then back to the one to turn him off!

13. Energy! What do we even mean by the word? Somewhere along the line, in Western parlance, we adopted the idea of a nervous system instead of an energy system. So, we started to equate energy with ideas like nervousness, anxiety, and mania.

14. That proved a fundamental mistake, one that we are still living with. Energy is different from states like anxiety, nervousness, obsession or mania. Energy is that mysterious vitality that distinguishes life from not life and living from hardly living.

15. Consider. When you despair, your energy dissipates. Where did your energy go? You had all sorts of energy … and then you didn't. How can a mental state like boredom or despair possibly drain the body of physical energy? What is going on there?

16. You might think that this subject is incidental to living. But consider life challenges like anxiety, depression, addiction, mania, chronic fatigue, and so on. What if these are

as much about energy regulation as about anything medical?

17. You heat up water in a boiler. You create steam. You give the boiler no way to release that steam. The boiler explodes. Is that too mechanical an explanation of explosive, impulsive or manic behavior? Or might that be close to what is actually going on?

18. Life is certainly different from non-life. But what is that basic difference? The salient difference between an amoeba and a rock is that one is animated and the other isn't. Something that is alive is animated and possesses energy. Life is energy.

19. Motorizing a toy truck doesn't bring that toy to life, except metaphorically. Its engine allows it to move, bump into chair legs, and so on. But life is different from that and more dynamic than that. Life energy is different from engine combustion.

20. But different how? Is anything more important to know and yet more confusing? How did human energy get all heated up in a manic person? Where did the energy go in a despairing person? Did it drain out? Or is it still stored somewhere, as in a battery?

21. And can it be that every human being comes into the world with exactly the same amount of animation, energy, and life force, creating the exact same consciousness? Or are some human beings fundamentally more electric and energetic?

22. We have no way of quantifying human energy or speaking sensibly about human energy. But it stands to reason that each of us must possess our unique amount:

sixty horsepower, a hundred horsepower, two hundred horsepower, who knows what?

23. What might that range be? And what qualitative differences might arise from differences in energy and life force? Might a person with too little life force reach too simple conclusions? Might a person with a grand life force overflow with ambition?

24. Most of these questions we must set aside as imponderables, as just too speculative to consider. But some we must come to grips with, as they are fundamental to our understanding of who we are, how we operate, and how we might choose to be.

25. For a philosophy of life to do its job, it must deal with the idea of life energy and the reality of life energy. What sort of thing is it? How can we increase it? How can we tame it? How can we store it? How can with live with too much of it or too little of it?

26. Is there a sense in which we can make full use of our genetic animation, whatever its amount, and live a more animated life rather than a less animated life? And, on balance, given the challenges we can predict, would that actually be a good thing?

27. Would it be a good thing to maximize the use of our life force? Let's say that a given car could travel at two hundred miles an hour. Would it be a good thing for it to be driven that fast for an extended period of time? Or would that destroy it?

28. It would matter whether it was built to travel at that speed for only short periods of time, maybe straining even then and maybe threatening to do itself damage, or

whether it was built to race along at top speed for extended periods of time.

29. It would matter how important it was for you to make use of that car's top speed. If you were hurrying to the hospital with an injured child, that would be one thing. But what if it were only for joyriding or because you had an impulse to go fast?

30. These are our questions. Kirists do not dodge them, even if they can't answer them. It is our job to speculate about them, ponder them, and think about them. See that young kirist under that oak tree? Maybe an apple is about to fall!

31. Consider intensity. Intensity is a high energy state where our energy is all potentiality or where it is doled out very carefully, in the service of an intention. That tremendous energy is gathered and then, at some point, explosively expended.

32. A racer is at the starting line. All that energy is gathered and marshaled. The starting gun is fired. Off! He was intense to begin with but he kept all that energy in check. He is intense now and expending that energy. Think about that sequence.

33. You intend to live your life purposes. Not only that, you intend to live them intensely. Feel that intensity, that energy. Where is it coming from? From your brain? Your heart? Your intentions? Your desire? Whatever its source, *you* are generating it.

34. A tennis player is about to serve. All of her energy is gathered and marshalled. But she tosses the ball into the air very carefully, even gently. That toss isn't where she uses

all that stored energy. If she did, she would throw it a mile high!

35. Even with all that marshaled energy and high intensity, that tennis player can still do a careful, controlled, calm thing. That is quite a feat, when you think about it. All that energy pulsing through your body and still you can toss a ball in the air calmly.

36. Someone with the passion and intensity of a Winston Churchill could still sit quietly and paint. It is no contradiction or paradox that a creature with a ton of energy may also be the stillest of creatures. Picture a tiger crouching. Soon she will be all energy!

37. Now the tiger is perfect stillness. She is still because she has her reasons. It isn't an abstract matter for her, about "balancing energy with stillness." She is still so that the antelope doesn't see or hear her. She is still so that she can have some dinner.

38. We, too, even if we have kilowatts of energy, must know how to be still and stay still, not as an abstract matter, not for the sake of something called balance, but because we can't write our novel or save the world if we are bouncing off walls.

39. Kirists muse on this. Imagine feeling a ton of energy in your being but your job is to sit still and write your novel or compose your symphony. It can be done: control and calmness are possible. But isn't all that pulsating energy a real challenge?

40. Can you feel how that pulsating energy almost cries out for a distraction, almost demands that you jump up and expend some of that energy? How can you write your

novel if you are on the verge of an explosion and hardly able to sit still?

41. And what if you are downright afraid of that intensity? What if you're rattled by your own energy? How can you live as a passionate person if that buzzing unnerves you? How can you fight for a cause if you are at war with your own energy?

42. Say that you grew up with a tyrant for a parent. Internally, you raged against him. The energy of hatred filled your body. Now, whenever energy starts to flow in you, it conjures that hatred and that tyranny. Aren't you bound to fear your own energy?

43. It turns out that it's completely possible to stand in unfortunate relationship to one's own energy. What then? In that case you would want to inaugurate a daily practice to help tolerate that energy. That would amount to energy wisdom at work!

44. And what about states of high alert? States of vigilance? All that energy gathered to make sure that you can still see your child playing on the monkey bars. Suddenly she's gone. Where did she go? Shock waves, electric current, adrenalin, energy!

45. So, it is completely possible to both crave intensity and to fear intensity. Think of that movie we have all seen a million times. An allied spy, dressed as a German officer, is dropped behind enemy lines. He has a vital mission, an unparalleled mission.

46. The very outcome of the war hinges on his success. We sit on the edge of our seat. Everything is heightened: when he snaps a twig, we jump a foot. When a light comes on,

we stop breathing. All of our energy is balled up, just as is all of his energy!

47. We want to be him, living that intensely, living out such an important mission. And at the same time, we absolutely don't. Such are the contradictions that make understanding human energy and managing human energy such a complex affair.

48. Our life purposes drive us to high intensity. That very intensity startles us, frightens us, wears us down. So, we return to a more inert state—and now we aren't living our life purposes. Now we feel low energy. So, we try to wake ourselves up again!

49. Even if we want to live intensely, can we? How are we to get from our ordinary state to that heightened state? Just by wishing it? Can we really generate intensity, passion, energy, and additional life force just by saying, "More energy, please"?

50. That Allied spy is in a set of circumstances that demands intensity. But are we? Does your commute demand intensity? Does sending out emails at work demand intensity? Is much of anything calling to you or driving you to a heightened state?

51. We expend energy all day long. We use up calories. But that is hardly the same thing as intensely living our life purposes, as generating a ton of energy in the service of powerful intentions and then having to deal with the energy we roused into being.

52. Or what about passion, that amazing energy state? We pay lip service to "wanting more passion." But do we really want to light ourselves up so that we glow in the dark? Do

we really want to live that intensely and deal with those consequences?

53. You observe the headstrong, egocentric, obsessive, heroic passion of a Beethoven or a Van Gogh and you think, "Yikes! I'm not up for that!" You announce that you are for calmness, tranquility, serenity. Then you discover that you feel listless.

54. No wonder we go up and down, up and down! We are on such an energy rollercoaster that we can easily talk ourselves into the belief that all forms of energy are dangerous. Uncontrolled mania may well be dangerous but is passion that dangerous?

55. We talk ourselves right out of passion, not wanting to get on that energy rollercoaster. We train ourselves not only to avoid displays of passion but the very feeling of passion and so settle for a life of safety, one that does not satisfy us in the slightest.

56. Kirists understand these dangers. They understand that they had better risk passion, for the sake of their life purposes and their self-obligations, even if that means riding a wild energy rollercoaster that leaves them breathless and shaken.

57. Ah, but what about the flip side? What if you have too little energy? That's what millions of people experience. Is that natural endowment? A medical issue? Trying circumstances? Formed personality? Or some sort of theft in childhood?

58. Well, we know some things. Do we experience more energy when life feels meaningful or when life feels meaningless? You know that the experience of meaningless is an

energy drain. But how can that be? How are meaning and energy related?

59. Well, consider. A neglected baby will first react energetically by crying and crying. But if she continues to be ignored, she will begin to lose her energy until she is practically inert. We call that "failure to thrive." Deeply demoralized, she may even die.

60. Kirists think about that. Maybe a given person's low energy is a direct result of her demoralization. Like that neglected infant who has failed to thrive, maybe she, too, is not thriving. No doctor can help her. She needs a completely revitalized life.

61. Human things reduce human energy. Being sick reduces our energy. Likewise, demoralization. Likewise, boredom. Likewise, regrets. Likewise, forced marches. Likewise, subjugation. Our energy supply is held hostage to our experience of life.

62. There is a direct relationship between what is going on in our mind and our energy supply. Even the most innocent thought can rob us of energy. We have an idle passing thought about the lawn needing mowing—and suddenly we feel exhausted.

63. Energy can drain away, just like that. And energy can also get hooked. We have all this energy: but instead of marshaling it, we turn it over to a worry, a fear, a craving, an obsession with the latest video game, social media, or television series.

64. Our energy can and does get hooked, squandered, stolen. Think of obsession, that high energy state where our energy gets hooked on a worry. Think of that peculiar

high energy state called mania that steals a thousand kilowatts of our energy.

65. Our life force is easily lost and easily squandered. And what if you have constitutional low energy? Then you have very little energy to lose or squander! How much energy are you wasting on that powerful compulsion? Maybe all the energy you have.

66. What if you need more energy? Where will it come from? You can't go down to the local market and buy a bunch of it, as you can radishes. You can't go to some energy bank. Kirists know that this is one of those questions they must stop and answer.

67. And if it can't be answered perfectly, maybe we can at least do a better job of inventing part-solutions. What about creating a simple visualization that provides us with the sense that energy is more in our control? Might that help a little?

68. Picture an "energy container." What if you mentally created such a container, deposited a ton of energy into it, and then withdrew energy when you needed it, say to live passionately, to live intensely, and to live aligned with your life purposes?

69. Visualize that container any way you like. Visualize it as an over-sized purse. Visualize it as a toy bank or maybe as something a bit larger, like Fort Knox. Visualize it in a customary way, as an alkaline battery. Dream up an energy container that suits you.

70. Say that you have an arduous task coming up. You go to your energy bank. You withdraw as much energy as you need. Now you stand ready. All that energy is available;

and, because it is available, you feel more equal to the task, readier to face it.

71. Maybe you have a difficult conversation looming ahead of you. You pull out your purse, push aside your lipstick and your comb, and retrieve some hundreds of watts of energy, just as much as you need, with maybe a few more thrown in for good measure.

72. Maybe your storage container is the tiniest of batteries, an amazing bit of nanotechnology, a battery only some molecules thick. Or maybe it looks more like a flashlight battery. Or maybe more like a generator. Or maybe more like a powerhouse!

73. Now this battery, like all batteries, might drain over time. So, you would need to recharge it. What sort of practice might that look like? We know the common phrase "recharge your batteries." But what might it look like to recharge your battery?

74. We have hardly begun to explore one of the most vital features of human existence, our life force. Some cultures have thought about this for thousands of years. But contemporary thinking is needed. Our approaches so far just aren't rich or wise enough.

75. Imagine if we really understood what blocks energy and what releases energy? Imagine if we could fathom the relationship between personality and energy? Then we could engage in a personality upgrade to increase and release our energy!

76. Imagine if you had a way of preventing energy from flowing toward an addiction, an obsession, a compulsion, or a mania? Maybe your strong, leak-proof energy

container could do that work! Wouldn't it be amazing if you could refuse them energy?

77. Or, if energy did head in their direction, what if you knew what to do to prevent it from getting hooked? Energy approaches a worry, threatening to energize it into an obsession. But you open a trap door or a French window and the energy zips on by!

78. Energy wisdom means all of this and so much more. Imagine if we knew how to store energy, control energy, replenish energy, free energy, apportion energy, modulate energy, and all things energy-related? Wouldn't that change our lives?

79. Energy wisdom means wondering what a loss of energy might signify. Kirists aren't quick to presume that a loss of energy is purely a physical matter. Couldn't it have something to do with past trauma, current sadness, or who knows what? We wonder.

80. Energy wisdom means taking as much control of our energy as we possibly can, so that we can produce it at will when we need it and control it when we begin to run too hot or too fast. We announce, "One of my practices is regulating my energy."

81. Energy wisdom means understanding that you might run a race and feel energized or you might run it and feel exhausted. And you might feel energized today and exhausted tomorrow! Let us not be too surprised or stand confounded by energy events.

82. The same with a lecture, a conversation, or a celebration. The exact same event might energize you one day and exhaust you another day, depending on everything

from your health to your mood. Kirists come to understand this rollercoaster reality.

83. Kirists number among their self-obligations the obligation to understand their own life force. A mechanic would not last a day if he avoided learning about engines. Let us rise to the occasion and dedicate ourselves to better understanding human energy.

84. We do this not for abstract reasons but for ethical reasons. If we see it as our job to do the next right thing and the right thing after that, we need energy for those undertakings. That makes bettering our relationship to energy a moral imperative.

85. We aspire to energy wisdom. We'll never fully acquire it, as our understanding of energy will always be limited. But we can aspire to it; we can pay real attention; and, through practice, maybe we can even learn to excel at energy management.

14

BOOK XIV. THE WORLD AND SORROW

1. A philosophy of life must also be a philosophy about the world. It must demand of itself that it address how society and culture operate, what forces align against the individual, and how each individual might want to relate to that messy, pressing reality.

2. It must likewise be real and true-to-life about circumstances. Human beings are not free to ignore quarantines, market crashes, cruel parents, persecutions, earthquakes, industry closures, or eight-month winters. Our circumstances matter.

3. As kirists try to make sense of their relationship to the world, they are confronted by the sobering reality that the world is not a daydream. They can't spin it out for their own amusement. Yes, it can be as beautiful as flowers; but it can also be as hard as nails.

4. That hardness leaves kirists shaking their heads. What is a kirist supposed to do about climate catastrophes, the reappearance of plagues, shameless greed, religious

warfare, fender benders, and pimples appearing on the morning of prom night?

5. What are we supposed to do? Kirism returns us to certain first principles: that we demand of ourselves that we make life purpose choices and strive to live our life purposes, even as we are forced to take the world and all of its arrows into account.

6. That is, we try. But we can't judge beforehand if our efforts will work. Will they provide us with the experience of meaning? Will they prove ethical? Will they match our hopes? We make a choice and hand that choice over to the world, which tests it.

7. We make decisions based on our understanding of the world, and, far too often, the world informs us that we've gotten the picture wrong. We thought that this or that plausible pursuit would prove a meaning opportunity—and it didn't.

8. You decide on a life in the world of non-profits. Don't non-profits support excellent causes? You start out enthusiastic and find yourself quickly resigned to the fact that your non-profit is authoritarian, sanctimonious, ineffective, and dull as dishwater.

9. You become a public defender so as to help the defenseless and the innocent. You burn out in two years because of your large caseload and the unjustness of the system, having, in the process, put on forty pounds from mindless over-eating.

10. You're an actor. You get a huge break and get to star in a silly movie that supports fairy tale thinking and costs $500,000,000 to make. To assuage your guilt, you donate

your salary to charity. And here comes your next equally silly opportunity …

11. You are born into a time, a town, and a family that hates who you are. They hate the look of you, your very nature, your very existence. You do not know this at first—for the first year or two of your life you're able to laugh and smile. Then you aren't.

12. The world is our albatross, not our oyster. As a child, you don't quite know this. You hear homilies and learn the rules of your culture. At the same time, you look out at the world and can't help but wonder if you aren't being sold a bill of goods.

13. Picture a clear-eyed seven-year-old. She has questions that she maybe doesn't dare ask. How can it be that millions of children are starving? Why are people homeless? Why do her parents pretend that a fat man is bringing her presents at Christmas?

14. If she does dare ask, what humbug will she be told? She sees the world with her own two eyes and she also receives the world via a million messages with which she is bombarded. This makes her deeply cross-eyed. And sorrow commences.

15. Because the world can be hard as nails, because our efforts to live our life purposes regularly fail, because we quickly learn about loss, injustice, humbug, impermanence, and death, there is no help for us: sorrow will live between the lines of life.

16. You will experience sorrow. You are a human being and all human beings experience sorrow. And, being human, you'll experience sorrow at the very oddest

moments, say when life is quite good or when something unusually excellent happens.

17. Life can be good. Life can be rich. Life can even sometimes exceed our expectations. But even at such moments, and often especially at such moments, feelings of sorrow, melancholy and regret invade us, almost as if they have something to teach us.

18. That a given moment can be at once wonderful and sorrowful speaks to the real, raucous, layered nature of now. Now is no simple thing. Nature did not build us to just peel a potato. It built us to know about death even as we smile, kiss and hug.

19. You hold your child's hand and experience a wonderful moment. Suddenly you're sorrowful. You're confronted by the inevitable passage of time and by the knowledge of all that your child will be obliged to experience, the bad with the good.

20. You are invaded by the knowledge of the impermanence of life. That touch of flesh provokes that knowledge and tears start flowing. They aren't happy tears. They are the tears of sorrow that want to well up when we are reminded of what life brings.

21. That is how "now" works. Kirists know this. They know that painful thoughts and feelings are always hovering nearby, ready to drop into the moment. Sorrows don't live far across town. They live just off to the side of every moment, waiting.

22. Since kirists know this, they try to prepare themselves for the layered, perplexing, disturbing reality of now. They ready themselves, smiling a small smile and exclaiming,

"Okay, now! Disturb me! Confound me! Confuse me! I get you!"

23. As a result of their preparations, kirists come to understand the nature of sorrow. They know that sorrow is not "depression." They know that sorrow is the song of a world in mourning, a world mourning its injustices, its tragedies, its very nature.

24. There is also something about love wrapped up with sorrow, and also something about compassion. Sorrow is part sadness but "sadness" does not capture the special quality of sorrow. Sorrow is something like the embrace of a long-lost comrade.

25. We celebrate our comrade's return while mourning all those lost years. Love and sadness, happiness and grief are all mixed together. Maybe sorrow is a teaching feeling. Why would nature do that? Maybe so that we live with our eyes wide open.

26. The pain of sorrow, which we do not crave and which we do not want, is maybe like the pain that tells us that our hand is too near the fire. Maybe it is crucial for our wellbeing. We do not love such reminders but maybe we need that reminding.

27. Holding our child's hand, feeling the pain of it as well as the joy of it, we are reminded of what we have and what we will lose. That experience of sorrow resets our compass and, as a result, we decide to bake cookies or go out for ice cream.

28. Had we not felt that sorrow, we might have been inclined to do the laundry or clean up the living room. But because we got that whiff of mortality, we decided that

baking cookies was our way to love. Sorrow invited in love and we decided to love.

29. Sorrow is such a complicated feeling, because part of what we're experiencing is our love of life. We feel sorrow because we can love, because we have loved, and because we can still love. Maybe sorrow only comes to someone who still loves life?

30. But that doesn't mean that we invite it. Sorrow may be "good for us" but it is also an anchor that can drag us into the depths of despair. It does not feel good and we do not want it. To that, nature says, "Ha!" and readies its piercing arrows anyway.

31. You read your guidebooks in anticipation of your six-month sojourn in Paris, where you'll be strolling the streets and writing in cafés. You grow giddy with anticipation. You arrive. You walk down some charming street. And suddenly you feel sorrowful.

32. You couldn't be happier. But you also couldn't feel lonelier. Something is tugging at your heart and angling you toward despair. You anticipated a beautiful experience and it is indeed a beautiful experience. But inexplicably it's also a mournful one.

33. What are you feeling as you walk down that Parisian street? Is it something about the nature of beauty, about how beauty can mesmerize us and seduce us? The street is everything that it ought to be but are we somehow being fooled by its beauty?

34. Might it be something about the Jews rounded up from this very street and deported to their deaths? Is it something about humanity's horrors, about collaborators, about

neighbors betraying neighbors, about unbearable malice and enmity?

35. Is it something about the philosophers who lived hereabouts who were sometimes such eloquent thinkers and often so weak as people? Is it something about the vast distance between people as they are and people as we wish they would be?

36. Is it that you've been reminded that you can't bottle this, that you can't keep this, that this is just a passing moment and that you must find a job when you return home and that probably it will be an awful one? Has "now" already become "tomorrow"?

37. Or maybe it is partly regret. Nature provides regrets. We walk down that Parisian street, feeling the psychological experience of meaning, and at the same time we hear ourselves say, "You idiot, you could have had this twenty years ago!"

38. "Now" is always ripe for regrets. We feel proud that we are loving our child so well. An instant later, we hear ourselves say, "Why didn't I stand up for my little sister against that bullying father of ours?" Regrets are right there, all around us, waiting.

39. The world creates sorrow. Circumstances create sorrow. The human experience creates sorrow. And human societies and cultures create sorrow. A philosophy of life must concern itself with human society, since everyone lives in its confines.

40. There is the world of plagues, typhoons and earthquakes: the natural world. Then there are the man-made worlds of society and culture. Those man-made worlds can

be as venomous as a snake, as restrictive as a prison cell, as relentless as a tsunami.

41. Societies are authoritarian by nature and by habit. Kirists are anti-authoritarian by nature and by habit. Even if they have made the decision to fit in, kirists are likely to find themselves in a tense, adversarial relationship with their own society.

42. This produces all sorts of difficulties and its own full measure of sorrow. It makes us sad that society is what it is and not a more welcoming place. It aggrieves us that we can't just love it and embrace it and that it can't just love us and embrace us.

43. A kirist has three basic choices: to blend in, to remain aloof, or to stand up. If she decides to blend in, her acquiescence makes her sad. If she decides on aloofness, her alienation makes her sad. If she decides to stand up, society's retribution makes her sad.

44. She would love to stand up. But she understands that, if she does, she will be punished. She will be read the riot act. She will be fired, sued, tormented, hunted. The history of the species tells a single tale: dispute society and pay the consequences.

45. Society is no benign thing. Nations, tribes, work cultures, fraternal organizations, religious sects, communes, country clubs, towns, neighborhoods, stand poised to judge their members, silence their members, and ostracize their members.

46. Can you plot your escape from society and culture? You will discover that you can't. How, for instance, will you get sufficient funding for your science lab if you don't play

the game of grant proposals and if you don't kowtow to funders?

47. How will you travel from here to there without those travel documents that societies demand, those passports, visas and identity cards? Could there ever be a world where you are free to roam and not be fettered by society's rock-hard borders?

48. I wrote some unflattering things about the mental disorder paradigm. What happened? The organization tasked with protecting the prestige, status and income of mental health providers threatened me with civil and criminal sanctions.

49. I wrote some unflattering things about gods. What happened? Law enforcement officials singled out my writings as the reading material of certain church firebombers they'd just arrested, failing to mention their other reading material, like the bible.

50. Briefly working in a government job, I thought it would be right to do more rather than less in the service of the veterans I was helping. I was informed by my bosses in no uncertain terms that doing more was completely unacceptable.

51. Briefly teaching at a university, I made my thoughts known at faculty meetings. I rather doubted that we were doing the best job we could be doing of serving our students. I described certain easy-to-make improvements. I wasn't rehired.

52. You've had your experiences, too, and you know that they've infiltrated your system and brought you sorrow. When you take even a single step, you find yourself in this

or that culture, with its secret handshakes, ironclad rules, and swift punishments.

53. You can't escape culture. Even trappers in the wild have their rules, their tensions, and their culture. Even a lone trapper and the beaver and otter he traps have their culture! We know this; we live this; we experience this; and sorrow follows.

54. We know this. But we can also be made to forget. Mass culture is a brilliant hypnotic mechanism excellent at entrancing us and soothing us into forgetfulness. That beautifully-made television series just about makes us forget that we are living in poverty.

55. Every culture creates a cultural trance that hypnotizes its citizens, soothes them, and ensnares them. Folks around the water cooler are hypnotized into talking about that new hit television series and not about rebellion or revolution.

56. A kirist is bound to get caught up in the same cultural trance affecting everyone. Maybe she'll fall in love with a Disney movie. Maybe she'll crave techno-gadgets. Maybe she'll choose a prestigious profession that supports the status quo.

57. How could she not? Culture is the air she breathes, it is everywhere around her, it spreads into corners and slips between seconds, it is messaging her, commanding her, bathing her. It is cajoling her silence, her money, and her allegiance.

58. Even though we understand how culture is created and what its objectives are, we can still fall for it just like the next person. That we both understand this and are too often duped and seduced by culture disappoints us and deepens our sorrow.

59. Kirists can fall for well-made fairy tales. Kirists can crave comfort and prestige. Kirists can prefer tenure to ostracism, year-end bonuses to whistle-blowing, security to daily warfare with the powerful. The why of all that is obvious enough.

60. This can produce an almost constant tension in a kirist's psyche. She wants to watch that slick new show. But she knows that she shouldn't. So, she throws out her television. Then she buys a new one, because she misses being entertained. Life!

61. The world is like that. As we decide on our life purpose choices, as we make our meaning investments and seize our meaning opportunities, as we create and honor our self-obligations, as we engage in our absurd rebellion, we must factor in the world.

62. We know that a day of plague is not like any other day. We know that a profession that sounds ideal may prove spotty in the flesh. We know that our own personality is susceptible to the blandishments of society. We know to factor in the world.

63. How do we factor it in? Do we think a thought and then add, "And what about the world?" Yes, we do exactly that, subtly, silently, and consistently. We stay alert, as part of our efforts to function in as clear-eyed and life-prepared a way as we can.

64. Comfort is not in the cards. The world does not provide ease and comfort and our efforts to remain alert will hardly relax us. Such vigilance! But it is a vigilance that we demand of ourselves. It is one of our necessary self-obligations.

65. If you love fairness, justice, freedom and goodness, you

will never fit comfortably into society. Your boss treats everyone cruelly. Will you just smile? Will you smile and smile and keep on smiling? Or will you sorrowfully but adamantly resist?

66. And so, we arrive at the sorrow of the freedom fighter. A kirist knows that her ethical sense will pit her against her culture and her society. She understands the absurdity of fighting such an unequal fight but she also knows exactly why she is fighting.

67. She may be able to find allies. She may be able to find cultural companions, like-minded warriors, other lone kirists. But, still, every morning she will wake to her world —to a storm, to a culture clash, to a seduction—and she will wake up to that all alone.

68. She will wake up as a freedom fighter wakes up in occupied territory, committed, anxious, and sorrowful, with bravery forced upon her. She will sit up, take a deep breath, and swing out of bed, planting her feet on her rug and in the world.

69. Kirists understand the world, understand resistance and understand the sorrow of the freedom fighter. They do not call this sorrow "depression" or act like their challenge is biological and the answer is chemical. They know better than that.

70. We could draw a picture of a beautiful world and we strive to make this recalcitrant world that beautiful one. We aim to increase its goodness, its fairness, its wisdom. We march in that direction, maybe with some comrades. That's the kirist agenda.

71. We have intimations of paradise, glimpses of heaven-on-earth. Paradise is a healthy baby born into a happy

family. Heaven-on-earth is freedom, friendship, a soft cheese and a crusty roll. We could easily draw that picture, if only the world would let us.

72. But instead the world gives us genetic abnormalities, angry parents, and political tyrannies. It gives us pandemics and mindless cruelties. It gives us this group pitted against that group. Sorrow comes and we cry dry-eyed.

73. The world gives us despondency. Yes, we can also have joys and pleasures. We can rise up, feel proud, sing songs. We can pass some time in trance, consuming culture's relaxations. But there the world is again, deflating us, demeaning us, constraining us.

74. Imagine a fifteen-year-old struggling with his world. His world is home, high school, the Internet, mass culture, texts, constant news, plus all the cataclysmic events that affect him: a rash of suicides, a rash of school shootings, a rash of expectations.

75. He is sorrowful. Call it despondent. Call it melancholic. Call it down. What he is not is "depressed," if by that we mean that he is having a problem with his hormones, his genes, or his neurotransmitters. The world has made him despondent.

76. What should we invite him to do? How can we help him? We can take him fishing for the weekend or enlist him in a project to get his mind off the world. But most crucially we can invite him to become a philosopher, to learn and absorb kirism.

77. We can paint him a picture of how to live in this exact world, with its precise difficulties. We can help him understand why it is his obligation to stand up, to absurdly rebel

against the facts of existence, to identify and then to live his life purpose choices.

78. He is just fifteen, after all. He will have a lot on his mind. Much of it will feel obsessive: pimples, video games, the girl who isn't giving him the time of day, the car he wants, the band he'd love to start, the way his grades aren't what they should be.

79. He keeps his headphones on to drown out his parents' fights. In his peripheral vision, he sees that the polar icecaps have melted further. Then there is the teacher who has it in for him. And the pimples! And so much Spanish vocabulary homework!

80. Into this obsessive, claustrophobic, melancholy world we drop hints about his obligations, his choices, and his path as a kirist. Maybe kirism will ring a bell with him or maybe it won't. Either way, we pry him from his video games and invite him to think.

81. We invite him to think about the world. It is not an invitation he is usually offered. What he is usually offered are trailers for the blockbuster films coming at Christmas. We offer him something very different: a philosophy of life to chew on.

82. The world is inevitable. Sorrow is inevitable. That doesn't make life a strictly dark affair. But it does make it an enterprise crisscrossed by shadows. On some days those shadows will make for darkness. On other days, they will highlight the light.

83. You have a body, for better or worse. You have a personality, for better or worse. You have a mind, for better or worse. And you have a world, for better or worse. You

are lashed to it as if you were lashed to the mast of a schooner. And that hurts.

84. As kirists think about life and as they plot their course, they factor in the reality of the world. They do not call it hell and they do not fantasize about it being heaven. They know that it has sharp edges and sweet moments; and that it comes with sorrow.

85. During a sweet dream, we escape the world. How lovely a respite! There are the scents of flowers and the smiles of children. Wars end and waves of peace commence. But then we waken and the obdurate world returns, as it always does.

15

BOOK XV. JOYS AND PLEASURES

1. Philosophies of life naturally must focus on suffering. They must, because physical pain is real, despair is real, loss is real, tyrants are real, betrayals are real, toiling at work is real, disappointing ourselves is real, aging is real, and death is real.

2. For a philosophy of life to try to smile all that away would make it false on the face of it. But then we face the following trap: an honest philosophy of life that identifies all that suffering can easily forget that there is more to life than all that suffering.

3. There is more to life than suffering. That's why we possess words like joy, pleasure, happiness, exultation, gladness, glee, elation, euphoria, and ecstasy. Those words represent true things that are sometimes part of the human experience.

4. Of course, they are only sometimes a part. Not one of those words has ever come with an adjective like "constant" attached. But that doesn't make them meaningless

or irrelevant. Pleasure and joy irrelevant? Not to human beings.

5. And what if they are only punctuation marks rather than steady currents? A comma of pleasure and an exclamation point of joy rather than tidal waves of wonderfulness? All right, then. Maybe they are only that. But punctuation is something!

6. Language would be gibberish and life would be intolerable without punctuation. Imagine a steady stream of nothing-in-particular punctuated by absolutely nothing-at-all. We'd pull out our hair and fall over in a heap. We need exclamation marks!

7. As if a thing that happens only occasionally or even just once is not worth mentioning. Is your child's first step meaningless because it happened exactly once? Is your first kiss meaningless because it happened exactly once? No; not to our species.

8. Ah, but is your child's third step or ninth step quite the same thing? Do we get that same welling up? Do we feel our heart pierced? Well, we do feel something and we do still smile, but a first step is a first step. That is how our species experiences life.

9. As kirists, we are obliged to think smartly about these various words, about what they represent and what they signify. We need to distinguish pleasure from joy from happiness from ecstasy. We need to be smart, so as to know what to promote.

10. If we aren't smart, we might cavalierly name some things as pleasures and then chase after them. Don Juan chases sex as if it could never let him down. Kirists know

better. We know that something is a pleasure only if it is experienced as a pleasure.

11. Nothing is a pleasure just by virtue of its nature, just as nothing is meaningful just by virtue of its nature. A thing is only pleasurable or meaningful if it is experienced as pleasurable or meaningful. How pleasurable is a snow cone in an ice storm?

12. Sex may often be a pleasure. But painful sex is not a pleasure. Unwanted sex is not a pleasure. Sex followed by regrets is not a pleasure. Sex as performance is not a pleasure. Sex may sometimes and even often be a pleasure, but it also may not.

13. Things are only pleasures contextually. That myth-making, that some something can always be a pleasure, can confuse us and prevent us from doing the wise thing, which is to create opportunities for pleasure, make investments in joy, and so on.

14. This mention of opportunities and investments should remind you of meaning. Meaning is like that, too: an experience is meaningful only if it is meaningful. That is why kirists talk about meaning opportunities and meaning investments.

15. These are sister ideas. Nothing is pleasurable unless it is experienced as pleasurable, nothing brings us joy unless it brings us joy, nothing makes us happy unless it makes us happy. Life does not come with "shoulds" but rather with "mights."

16. A beautiful day might make us smile. Or, if we are in a foul mood, it might not. A kiss might make us happy. Or, if it is part of an arranged marriage, it might not. A beautiful

day or a kiss might bring us some joy. Or they might do nothing for us.

17. Our first headline: something is a pleasure only if it is. Visiting your parents may be a pleasure. Visiting your parents may not be a pleasure. There is nothing intrinsically pleasurable about visiting your parents. Either it is pleasurable or it isn't.

18. This can really trouble and confound us, that a pleasure isn't a pleasure unless it is. When something that we presumed would prove a pleasure doesn't, how disappointed we can feel! What a mountain we can make out of that everyday occurrence.

19. This is one way that we make our own pain. We look forward to something, supposing that it will be a positive experience. It turns out that it isn't. Nothing remarkable just happened but because we took a certain outcome for granted, we got hurt.

20. There are no pleasure assurances, just pleasure opportunities and pleasure investments. How does this work in practice? You pick something that you've previously liked. You hope that it'll still prove pleasurable. But who knows? How could you know?

21. You stand ready to experience pleasure. No reason not to stand ready! But you're also easy with the possibility that you won't. Maybe there's a ninety percent chance that you'll experience pleasure. What lovely odds! But we factor in that ten percent.

22. Say that you've enjoyed reading mystery novels in the past. For this or that reason, you haven't picked one up in a while. So, you give a mystery a try. Will you still have a

taste for it? Will it hold your attention? Will it or won't it still prove a pleasure?

23. Who can say? You can only know by trying. You make an investment in this experience by locating a novel, finding a quiet spot to read, and reading. But you do not over-invest. You don't put your wellbeing to the test with this little experiment!

24. If you're in the habit of over-investing, you're likely to not even try reading that mystery. This might sound like, "I've so loved mysteries! I don't want to learn that I don't love them any longer! That would be tragic! So, I'm never reading one again!"

25. Headline one: something is a pleasure only if it is. Headline two: do not need this or that to prove a joy. You can hope that it will prove a joy, you can want it to prove a joy, but if you *need* it to prove a joy, you have set yourself up for all sorts of troubles.

26. If the experience proves pleasurable, bank it. First of all, enjoy it! Second, put it in your memory banks as an experience that you actually enjoyed. It is so important to know which of our experiences we've actually liked! Enjoy it and memory bank it.

27. If the experience proves neutral or negative, which will amount to a disappointment and, unless you are careful, even a kind of defeat, take that kirist step to the side and apply your awareness to the situation. Step to one side and think.

28. Murmur to yourself, "That was very interesting. I really quite expected that I would enjoy reading that mystery. And I didn't enjoy it at all. What happened, I wonder?

What 'didn't work'? And what might this experience have to teach me?"

29. It might mean that you can't read mysteries until you get your own mystery written, the one that you've put aside for a year. Maybe mystery-reading pleasure is being held hostage and can't be released until the ransom of your own mystery is paid.

30. It might mean that this particular mystery wasn't very good, that cozy mysteries are now too lightweight for you and that you need hardboiled mysteries, or that you landed on the killer so early that the rest of the mystery felt anti-climactic.

31. It might mean that until you attend to your life purposes, you do not have permission from yourself to be entertained. Maybe there is a cause that you know you ought to be supporting and that you've been avoiding. Well, this experience alerted you.

32. A rough formula: provide yourself with pleasure opportunities and make pleasure investments. If they produce pleasure, smile and cheer. If they don't produce pleasure, stop and think. Step to the side and review. This will increase your joy ten-fold!

33. What makes pleasure more likely? Awareness. There is a link between awareness and pleasure. You will experience more pleasure as you become wiser about what defeats pleasure, what stunts pleasure, and what promotes pleasure.

34. You enter a café where you intend to work on your novel. It is very noisy. You rather like noise, so you idly think, "I can write here." But in a corner of your mind you

know that this café is just too noisy. You override that awareness and take a seat.

35. Five minutes later, you hear yourself say, "I can't write today." You'd been anticipating a pleasurable hour with your novel and now you're crestfallen. If you don't identify that the noisy café thwarted you, you won't understand how to create pleasure.

36. Pleasure may well await you at a quieter café. That may be all that is required to turn this misstep into a joyous hour. The novel didn't fail you, cafés haven't failed you, life hasn't failed you. You simply sat down in a café that was too noisy.

37. So, find a quieter one. Pleasures are attainable in this way. You have a hunch: this might be pleasurable. You try it. If it is, that is splendid. If it isn't, you consider what happened. What a simple formula! Have a hunch, give it a try, then consider.

38. We consider; and we wisely decide to make investments in things that previously brought us joy. Did we used to enjoy mint chocolate chip ice cream? We invest in a pint. Did we used to enjoy suspense fiction? We take ourselves to the library.

39. Of course, we know that there is no guarantee that we are going to get joy from that ice cream or that novel. But aren't the odds on our side? The past does not predict the future but it certainly gives us something to go on!

40. We can punctuate our days with pleasure if we invest in prospective pleasures and seize opportunities for pleasure. But what about joy? Joy seems like a bigger deal feeling. If pleasure is like the warmth of the sun, joy seems more like a supernova.

41. Is joy available to human beings? Is joy real or is it some sort of invention or convention? What do you think? You will need to check in with yourself to see what you think. Have you ever experienced what you would call joy? If you have, it exists!

42. If you haven't, that doesn't prove that joy doesn't exist. Rather, that may mean that somewhere along the line you got robbed of your ability to experience joy. It may have gotten stolen by harm done to you in childhood. That theft frequently happens.

43. This leads to two headlines. First, if you've experienced joy, joy is therefore real and worth your time and attention. Second, if you haven't experienced joy, you might want to inaugurate a daily healing practice that, fingers crossed, leads at last to joy.

44. Say that you have experienced joy or, through healing, can now experience joy. What will provide that heart-warming feeling? Here are some reasonable candidates. They do not come with guarantees but they are worth considering as investments.

45. One candidate is beauty. Beauty is both a suspect word, as we can be seduced by beautiful things (like a glorious sunset caused by air pollution), and also as pure a word as we possess, as when some pigments on a canvas bring us unadulterated joy.

46. Another candidate is love. Aren't love and joy natural partners? If we opt to love, as opposed to standing back at arm's length and stonily observing the universe, won't we feel that warmth all through our body, that supernova of joy made real?

47. Another candidate is service. When, as a volunteer, we

care for an infant brought to an emergency care nursery and see that infant smile after all her crying, the joy we feel is immense. For one split second, we experience a warmth that is indescribable.

48. Another candidate is mastery. It can bring us joy that we have excelled at something. It can bring us joy that we did a hard thing well. If we both do the next right thing and also do it well, what more can we ask of ourselves? And some joy may follow!

49. Another candidate is creativity. Creativity is the word we use to stand for manifesting loves like writing, painting, singing, crafting, inventing, and so on. Spinning a yarn or spinning yarn are age-old joys that are still abundantly available to us.

50. Another candidate is intimacy. There is no joy like the joy of chatting quietly with an intimate. In that secure space, the world seems safer and saner. Yes, it is possible to choose the wrong intimates. But what a joy to secure a right one!

51. Another candidate is family. Maybe it isn't our birth family: maybe they are too difficult and not to our liking. Then we create family, where we lavish friendship, loyalty, and caring and from which we receive a real measure of joy and pleasure.

52. Any one of our life purposes is also a possible source of joy. To live our life purposes is to promote joy. And while those moments may be brief and few and far between, they are also our wealth. Those joyous moments are our human riches.

53. Our child marries. The ceremony is very brief. But those few minutes can be as rich as minutes can be. And,

somewhere within us, they last forever. How can you calculate the value of something that lasts a second but that also lasts forever?

54. Moments of joy, suddenly here and suddenly gone, are not just passing moments. They are momentous. So, we covet them, we prize them and we angle for them. And, if we rarely or never experience them, we step to the side and try to figure out why.

55. In kirism, we have available to us that step to the side, that step that we take to provide ourselves with time and space to practice awareness. How many more joys and pleasures might we experience if we stepped to the side and took careful stock?

56. Say that you've been living one of your life purposes, for instance writing your novel. You stop to make yourself a cup of tea. As the water boils, you might worry that what you just wrote was terrible; or you could feel joy at having honorably worked.

57. Imagine! There you are standing in the kitchen, waiting for the water to boil, and instead of beating yourself up about your last few paragraphs or shaking your fist at the publishing gods, you allow yourself a moment of joy at having written!

58. You just got a precious moment of joy by allowing for it. If you rarely allow for joy, what exactly is going to feel joyous? Will that delicious soup, if your mind is completely elsewhere? Will your child's sudden smile, if you are always in the other room?

59. Yes, more pleasures, please. More joy, please. More happiness, please. But we can't just pluck these out of thin air. How can we pluck joy out of a joyless marriage? So,

we treat these as we treat meaning: in terms of opportunities and investments.

60. You find yourself in a joyless marriage. Well, maybe you should just leave it. But perhaps you have your reasons for staying. If so, then you're obliged to invest in it. What might the two of you enjoy? Make as long a list as you can make and study it.

61. Far down the list is a weekend away. Even further down is walking side-by-side holding hands. But, as you sit with your list, you can feel those two rising. A weekend away, walking side-by-side, holding hands. Worth the investment?

62. You propose it. Your partner is surprised, skeptical, and pleased all at once. Already you are feeling the slightest tingle of joy. No, the universe has not magically shifted on its axis. But suddenly a bit more joy exists than did the second before.

63. You can't count on the weekend working. It is merely an opportunity. Are you confident? Maybe not. Has anything changed? Maybe not. But are you standing open to some pleasure, some joy, some happiness? Yes, you are.

64. Maybe nothing joyful will happen. But maybe something will. And then? Well, you repeat it. You take weekends away as ongoing opportunities for joy. You invest in them. Maybe you can't count on them but you can look forward to them!

65. Can we perhaps even elevate joy, pleasure, happiness and those sister words to the high place of life purpose? Ah, a good question. Because, can that possibly be ethical? Can doing the next right thing and being a hedonist coexist? Can that work?

66. Is it either ethical or plausible to live for pleasure? Probably not. That last slice of pizza might please us but if we're dieting we need to skip it. Sleeping with our neighbor might excite us but it would also betray our marriage. Our ethics come first.

67. So, we want pleasure. But it isn't plausible to raise it to the exalted place of life purpose. In fact, we may have to upgrade our personality to guarantee that we don't chase pleasure—and, as a result of that upgrade, we'll experience more pleasure!

68. When you upgrade your personality, you provide yourself with more opportunities for pleasure. Say that you're consumed by ambition. If so, won't it prove devilishly hard to experience helping another person or walking in nature as a pleasure?

69. But, say that you've managed to modulate that ambitiousness. Then lending a helping hand might bring you joy. A nature walk might warm your heart. You would no longer race past possible pleasures and no longer stand immune to everyday pleasures.

70. Joy, pleasure, satisfaction, happiness, elation, ecstasy: what important words! A kirist tries to make sense of each of these, feeling through their differences and arriving at a sense of what is available, what is desirable, and where to set the bar.

71. Take the word "ecstasy." We've likely experienced pleasure, joy and happiness. But what about ecstasy? We have the word but have we had the experience? Is ecstasy perhaps a word better suited to the world of wishful thinking?

72. A kirist is a little skeptical of states that seem to require

powerful drugs or visits from gods. If ecstasy is fantasy or the fruit of a chemical, it must surely be a different thing from pleasure, joy, and happiness. Can there be kirist ecstasy?

73. Well, let us allow for it! Forget about trance dancing, magic mushrooms, or tantric sex. What if the very act of living a kirist life created ecstatic experiences? Let us leave that possibility wide open, either for us or for future generations.

74. And now: the word "happiness." Happiness is such a difficult word! It connotes something steady and long-lasting, as in "a happy life." But we also speak about moments of happiness. Is happiness more like a particle or more like a wave?

75. We know that we can have moments of happiness, just as we can have moments of joy or pleasure. We can even have days of happiness, maybe even weeks of happiness. But does the idea of "a happy life" put us at odds with our intentions?

76. Kirists opt for absurd rebellion. We assert our individuality. We are adamant about living our life purposes, no matter how much work they make. We know to do the next right thing and the right thing after that. Can all this and happiness coexist?

77. Maybe. But what we know is that we mustn't chase happiness. Our self-obligation is to do what we need to do in order to live a life that makes us proud. If we are then also gifted with happiness, that must be the very pinnacle of human existence.

78. Imagine that lucky combination, living a full, rich kirist life and also experiencing happiness. Indeed, you might

even make that one of your kirist practices, to envision a rich, intentional kirist life that is also a happy life. That is worth picturing!

79. Pleasures are possible. Satisfactions are possible. Joys are possible. Moments of happiness are possible. And maybe, with great luck, we can even approach something that must be the ideal: a proud kirist life that is also a happy life. Who knows?

80. But we do not chase happiness as if it were a bright shiny object. We do not chase anything. We stand up, we do the next right thing, but we do not chase. And all that not chasing produces a state which is itself a joy and a pleasure: serenity.

81. As we live our kirist life, doing what needs to be done, setting and meeting our self-obligations, experiencing joys, pleasures, and our measure of happiness, and living our life purposes, we practice serenity and we may even be gifted with serenity.

82. But we don't chase it. Just as we don't chase happiness, joy, or pleasure, we don't chase serenity. We live our kirist life and, by virtue of living exactly as we know to live, we may be gifted with serenity. Serenity may find us without us chasing it.

83. A serene life punctuated by moments of pleasure, happiness, and joy is perhaps humanly possible and likely exactly what we want—just so long as we do not lose sight of our intentions, our self-obligations, and our pressing life purposes.

84. We possess a family of words that include pleasure, joy, and happiness. We embrace this much-to-be-desired family but we do not live for it. Rather, we see these experiences

as fortuitous punctuation marks in a life organized around our life purposes.

85. More joy, then! More pleasure. More happiness. Maybe even some ecstasy. Let's angle for them, coax them, and stand open to them. But first let us live proudly, doing the next right thing and aligning our life with our wisest intentions.

16

BOOK XVI. SUBVERSIVE INTIMACY

1. Intimacy can complement and support a kirist's life intentions. Indeed, the desire for intimacy and efforts in the direction of intimacy can amount to life purposes and self-obligations in themselves. Intimacy is one of those things worth valuing.

2. A useful philosophy of life should have its ways of speaking to that important human state of affairs, intimacy. It should have its ways of advocating for intimacy and its ways of helping kirists create their best intimate relationships possible.

3. But why advocacy? Certainly, it must be possible to live well alone or in the company of colleagues and friends? Couldn't one fulfill one's self-obligations, make oneself proud, and live a full kirist life without intimacy entering the equation?

4. Yes, one could. A lack of intimacy is nothing like a life deal-breaker. In fact, many kirists live alone, and for good reasons. But intimacy at its best is of real value and a wise

contemporary philosophy of life should spell out those benefits and virtues.

5. At the same time, that philosophy of life shouldn't mince words about the difficulties that inevitably arise when two people try to share a bed and a life. Those difficulties are real, grave and sometimes insurmountable. We must admit those hard truths.

6. Few people are spared relationship problems. Kirists are no different in this regard. There is nothing surprising about this. It is a myth that it ought to be easy for two people to live together in intimate relationship. That is advertising hokum.

7. It is likewise a myth that someone must be at fault if two people come together and subsequently separate. Relationships can fail simply because the partners do not possess sufficient reasons to share a bed, bodily fluids, and their innermost dreams.

8. This is true across cultures, in straight and gay relationships, and whether the couple is comprised of kirists or not. People can come together and then separate without anyone being at fault. It may be that they just had too few reasons to stay united.

9. Nowadays such folks have permission to separate. But for thousands of years, the divorce rate was kept artificially low by cultural injunctions against divorce and by cultural norms that painted marriage as the only right and proper option.

10. By vesting control in men's hands, by enacting laws limiting the grounds upon which a divorce could be sought, and through the myth-making of the troubadour

tradition, which romanticized love, even the most hellish marriages endured.

11. These artificial cultural and societal constraints forced unhappy couples to remain together and kept closeted the relationship problems that were indubitably there. Unhappy women were labeled hysterical; abuse flourished; and secrets were kept.

12. As freedom gained ground, as religion lost its iron grip, and as women secured rights and power, a time came when marriages had to stand on their own two feet if they were to survive. Between half and two-thirds of them couldn't and still can't.

13. It turns out that, if society doesn't step in to artificially shore them up, the majority of intimate relationships are likely to fail. The heat dwindles; irritations increase; differences of opinions stop seeming amusing. The house of cards topples down.

14. So, should we turn our back on the ideas of real intimacy and committed relationships? We absolutely shouldn't. Excellent relationships may prove rare; all may face their difficulties; but, if you get lucky, you will have achieved something exceptional.

15. Why lucky? Because you can't make a successful relationship happen on your own. You need an equal partner. You need someone who will make the same sorts of agreements and commitments that you make. You need luck in that regard.

16. So, it takes two. Your right significant other may not be the first person you meet. It may not be the tenth. It may take a marriage and a divorce before she comes strolling

into your life. And only with that person will there be sufficient reasons to be together.

17. If an intimate relationship is to stand the test of time, the individuals involved must have not just some reasons for staying together. They need sufficient reasons. This sets the bar uncomfortably high but there is really no other place to set it.

18. How should such a relationship look? When will it be worth it? Well, to begin with, a kirist would love her mate to be her friend, her lover, her partner, her soulmate. But she also has some other special—and mandatory—requirements.

19. She needs her mate to provide her with real freedom, the freedom to hold her own ideas, to make mistakes and messes, to spend time in solitude, and, in a sense which can stretch the fabric of any relationship, to live a genuinely independent life.

20. A kirist is an individual first. She has her own ideas, her own ideals, her own principles, her own self-obligations. If her relationship supports her autonomy, it is a benefit. If her relationship counters it or constrains her, it is an albatross.

21. She likewise needs her mate to be "in it" with her. This "being in it together" is different from love, from respect, from empathy, from caring, from compassion. It is a decision that two people make that they will face life together, shoulder-to-shoulder.

22. The two of you have made the decision to take the other person's side. You both have pledged to side with that person above all others. The love-making, the quiet

conversations, the like-mindedness, are frosting on that cake. Rock-solid solidarity is at the forefront.

23. You might conceive of this excellent relating as the creation of a subversive unit, a resistance cell deep inside occupied territory, where two like-minded partisans work to defeat a common enemy. That's how "in it" they are: they are in it completely.

24. There is only one marriage vow: you are the most important person in my life. When that changes, when the person you sleep with is not the most important person in your life, your subversive unit has again become just two individuals sharing a bathroom.

25. No legal document creates such a unit. No amount of love guarantees such a unit. It happens in a simple but rare way: two people shake hands and agree to become partisans. They agree, maybe without a single word having been uttered.

26. What does refusing to take the other person's side look like? Maybe you remember how the movie "Frida" opens? Frida Kahlo is taken from her deathbed and flamboyantly rushed to the opening of her first-ever one-woman show.

27. The show is a great success and Frida is triumphant. We are then transported back in time to Frida as a little girl and we watch her story unfold, a story that focuses on her relationship with the already world-renowned Diego Rivera.

28. The filmmakers would like us to believe that Frida and Diego, despite their ups and downs, despite Diego's incessant affairs and Frida's occasional ones, so loved and respected one another that their relationship must be judged successful.

29. Such is the Frida-and-Diego mythology. But the reality, which the movie inadvertently exposes, is that Diego refused to take Frida's side. Throughout their relationship, Diego tells Frida that she is a great painter. Yet he never secures her a show until the very end.

30. How can that be? How can Diego tell her to her face that she is a great painter and at the same time make no efforts behind the scenes to secure her a show? His affairs are only one betrayal. They pale in comparison to this greater betrayal.

31. Was he envious? Was it cruelty? Was it indifference? Whatever its source, Diego did not go to bat for Frida until she was on her deathbed. If Diego Rivera had really respected and loved Frida Kahlo, he would have done much more for her.

32. Despite his claims to love her work and despite his claims to love her, his actions announce that he was not really on Frida's side. Such failures define relationships. The passionate love-making, the zany festivities, all of that is just window-dressing.

33. For a relationship to reach the level that kirists require, each partner must give a serious damn about the needs of the other. Lip service won't do. Bouquets of roses after the fact won't do. Fine anniversary speeches won't do. That care must exist daily.

34. Well, and say that there are some decent reasons for two people to be together, even some excellent ones, but not really sufficient ones? What is likely to happen then? A settling. The couple will settle for what they do have—and that settling will have its consequences.

35. Maybe they will settle into a cool, distant relationship.

Picture two university professors living at either end of a railroad flat in some university town. They can talk circles around their lack of warmth without producing the least bit of kindness or heat.

36. Maybe they will settle into a dramatic relationship, where each partner feels unjustly treated and makes that dissatisfaction known. Dishes fly, accusations fly, and the very hysteria of the relationship keeps it together, all that noise acting as a kind of glue.

37. Maybe they will settle into a despairing relationship, where one or both partners feel emotionally and existentially under the weather. Maybe they will call this "depression" and maybe both will take antidepressants, settling for chemicals.

38. Or maybe a kirist will enter into one brief relationship after another, as her desire for intimacy collides with the fact that insufficient reasons exist for remaining with this or that partner. Maybe life will look like a series of so-so affairs.

39. Or maybe this settling will prove adequate. Maybe it will prove enough. Maybe it will prove palatable. Maybe the good reasons for being together will on balance feel just about sufficient. Maybe it won't feel like settling but like something better.

40. Or maybe it will prove impossible for a given kirist to just settle. If so, then the upshot may be spending long periods of time—months, years and even decades—alone. Not able to find someone genuinely "in it" with her, she decides not to settle.

41. All of these outcomes are possible: no relationships, decent enough relationships, strained relationships, and the

occasional excellent one. And what will characterize that excellent one? It will look like it has been built out of the following twenty building blocks.

42. Building block one: each partner cares for the other's solitude. It must be all right and more than all right that each partner gets to spend significant time pursuing his or her own activities and the requirements of his or her own inner life.

43. Building block two: the couple pays mindful attention to the maintenance of emotional security. Each partner is not only aware of the other's feelings but takes them into account and actively works to help his partner feel good rather than bad.

44. Building block three: the couple pays mindful attention to the maintenance of meaning. Partners understand that meaning comes and goes, that meaning crises happen, and that sometimes changes must be made for meaning to be restored.

45. Building block four: the couple pays mindful attention to the maintenance of passion. Partners will not let themselves become too busy for sex and love, too tired for sex and love, or too disinterested in sex and love.

46. Building block five: the couple aims to create at least occasional happiness. They ask questions of each other like "What would make you happy?" and alert their partner to their current needs by announcing, "This would make me happy."

47. Building block six: each partner demands discipline from himself and gently demands discipline from his partner. Each partner strives to work in a regular, undramatic

way on his or her life purposes, with few complaints, tantrums, or excuses.

48. Building block seven: partners engage in a gentle exchanging of the truth. When there is something that must be said, even if it's painful or embarrassing, it gets said, carefully, thoughtfully, and compassionately, but also clearly and directly.

49. Building block eight: both partners accept the limits of the human and the facts of existence. Each partner expects a lot from himself and his partner while at the same time accepting that failures of nerve and pratfalls do regularly happen.

50. Building block nine: partners strive to minimize their own unwanted qualities. Each partner will bravely look in the mirror, take a fearless personal inventory, and identify and then change those aspects of personality that harm the relationship.

51. Building block ten: each partner supports the other's dreams and ambitions, including his or her career ambitions. If a dream can't be supported—if, say, one dearly wants children and the other absolutely doesn't—that reality is put on the table.

52. Building block eleven: the couple maintains a real friendship. They share stories; they share memories, they share secrets; they laugh; they walk hand-in-hand; they smile at one another; and they shake their head at each other's hilarious antics.

53. Building block twelve: partners stay alert to their own moods and to the moods of their partner. Each partner will sometimes feel blue and despair may prove an unin-

vited guest in the relationship. The couple addresses sadness when it appears.

54. Building block thirteen: each partner accepts that the other may sometimes have a hard time of it. Each kirist is on his or her own rollercoaster ride, maybe caught again in a recurrent negative loop, and partners notice this—and offer assistance.

55. Building block fourteen: with luck, the couple will share values and principles. If they do, then their unit of two will prove a powerhouse. They will fight the same fights and take the same stands. If they don't, they know to expect that a reckoning is coming.

56. Building block fifteen: each manages his or her own journey. Each partner has the job of taking responsibility for his or her own life, for setting goals and for planning, for making choices and for taking action, and for proceeding as a responsible adult.

57. Building block sixteen: each partner communicates carefully. The two speak clearly, promptly, gently, and mindfully about all those large and small matters that continually arise and that, if not addressed, fester and breed misery.

58. Building block seventeen: the partners bring artfulness to the partnership. As creative people, they have a repertoire of talents: whimsy, imagination, meticulousness, and several dozen more. They bless their relationship with these talents.

59. Building block eighteen: they promptly let go of yesterday. Partners let go of past grievances, not so as to excuse them, not so as to invite more of them, not so as to lose

themselves in the relationship, but because they know the value of forgiveness.

60. Building block nineteen: partners treat each other fairly. They demonstrate fairness in everything large and small—by honoring agreements, by distributing resources equitably, and by not doing what they wouldn't want their partner to do.

61. Building block twenty: they invest time in their relationship. Even if they find it naturally easy to relate, even if both are "low maintenance," the two partners still know to pay real attention to this excellent thing that they have created together.

62. Does any intimate relationship look this good or work this well? Aren't human beings just a little too flawed, selfish, inflexible, opinionated, unaware, moody and grumpy to rise to this major occasion? Isn't this "subversive unit" idea just a pipedream?

63. The perfected example of it may be a pipedream. But decent approximations are possible. Kirists hold this vision of the high-bar goal of approximations of excellence not as wishful thinking but as their work, as their self-obligation, and as a possibility.

64. A high-bar goal for kirists is the creation by two ever-changing, completely human people of a bastion of safety and sanity in a dangerous world. It is the creation of nothing less than a tight-knit unit where each protects, supports, and respects the other.

65. It is good to have this picture of excellent relating. Kirism is an aspirational philosophy that invites each of us to do the next right thing, as difficult as that is, to retain

our individuality, as difficult as that is, and to relate beautifully, as difficult as that is.

66. Picture that fine relating. Each day you consider what your partner needs. Maybe it's the freedom to create. Maybe it's a bit of truth-telling. Maybe it's dinner out. Maybe it's you being there calmly and quietly as he goes through a hard time.

67. In turn, you tell him what you need, secure in the knowledge that he will listen. You know that he won't interrupt. You know that he won't roll his eyes. You know that he won't snicker. You know that the concern registering on his face is genuine.

68. You work to minimize your own unwanted qualities—your addiction, your unhealthy narcissism, your critical nature, your histrionics, your timidity, your lack of self-confidence, your arrogance, whatever it might be. This supports the alliance.

69. You make love. You laugh. You sit quietly. You watch a movie. You make plans. You remember the past. You handle a sudden challenge. You give each other time and space. When he or she drops your favorite coffee mug and breaks it, you offer a hug.

70. This picture of fine relating provides a blueprint and an ideal. And if you don't have this sort of relationship and suspect that you can't have it? Then, because this ideal is alive in your mind and circulates in your blood, you may miss it a lot.

71. You may even have to mourn for it and grieve over it. Kirism respects the truth that life comes with sorrow. We do not say that life is sorrow or that life is a cheat but we do

acknowledge that life comes with sorrows and that we can feel badly cheated.

72. If this grand relationship isn't in your cards, then you will have to coax meaning into existence in other ways. If it's currently eluding you, then you live your life purposes anyway, since even the absence of love doesn't absolve you of your self-obligations.

73. And, of course, you might still have it one day. Life isn't over. Maybe you don't want to search for it any more. Maybe you're tired of the whole thing. Maybe it's too sore a subject. But who knows what tomorrow or two years from now will bring?

74. And what about the intimate relationship you have right now? Can it be improved? Maybe currently you're in a relationship where you're just settling, which is leaving you irritable and despondent. But is there a chance for more?

75. You may have the intuition that there isn't, that what you have is all there is. Then you are obliged to bravely think through your options: to continue settling; to get out; or, despite your doubts, to make an effort to improve what you have.

76. You might work to upgrade your personality, to see if that makes a difference. You might take that kirist step to the side and bring your full awareness to the situation. You might create a daily relationship practice and invite your partner to join you.

77. My mother had an affair with a married man and I resulted. She loved him; he loved her; they talked of him divorcing and them marrying; but he gambled and

couldn't be trusted. She had many reasons to be with him, including me, but she ended it.

78. Relationships are like that. There may be kids. There may be bad habits, repeated betrayals, addictions. There may be ocean-wide gulfs or hot love that still can't burn away the imperfections. There may be minor grievances or huge objections.

79. And so, is intimacy worth it? You will have to decide for you and I will have to decide for me. If you decide that it is worth it and if you currently don't possess it, then that may prove a place of renewed absurd rebellion, rebelling against our basic aloneness.

80. You absurdly rebel by countering your own doubts, your own misgivings, and your earned reluctance and by giving intimacy that kirist thumbs-up gesture. Yes, the smile you're wearing may be a bit sardonic. But, still, the gesture is real.

81. As any true-to-life philosophy of life ought to do, kirism focuses on the lone individual acting like a lone individual and feeling like a lone individual. But that isn't the whole story. Kirists can also find themselves "in it" with other human beings.

82. And that may be the ideal. Facing life as two, in a relationship that is working, adds everything from warmth under the covers to a dinner companion to a second breadwinner to someone who gets your jokes and will laugh even at the abysmal ones.

83. You can live alone and thrive. You can be alone and flourish. But if the gods of whimsy smile down on you and on that other someone and allow the two of you to couple

and combine your forces, well, that is nice. That is very nice indeed.

84. May the two of you function like that subversive cell in enemy territory. May you drink up the wine so that it doesn't fall into enemy hands, may you sing songs of freedom, may you laugh at your private jokes. May you stand together!

85. Intimacy is more than just sex and shared secrets. An intimate relationship of the sort I've described is a true bastion of support and sanity in a challenging world. Each partner gains something profound and immeasurable.

17

BOOK XVII. THE MYSTERY DIVIDE

1. All human beings, and therefore all kirists too, fall into one or the other of two rough categories: those who have a taste for mystery and for whom "spirit" signifies something; and those who have a dislike of the word and see "spirit" as humbug.

2. This division is extremely rough, as a secular kirist and a spiritual kirist can be one-and-the-same person. She can be one on Monday and the other on Tuesday; or one when she is doing math and the other when she is going on a shamanic journey.

3. This division, while rough, is nevertheless real and as wide as a river. It is wide between people and wide within the same person. It creates perplexing problems for good-hearted kirists and produces in each of us a heightened sense of alienation.

4. Someone says to you: "The universe is love." A secular kirist will likely think, "That's superstitious nonsense." A

spiritual kirist may well think, "That's a deep truth." I'll have my unshakeable belief and you'll have yours. Neither of us can be budged.

5. We can't be budged because this is what we actually and actively believe. We believe it in our bones. The rationalist will say, "Use your head." The spiritualist will say, "Have faith." Having said that, we are just about done communicating.

6. We are done because there is no way to know one way or the other, no way to settle the matter, no experiments to run, no fact, example or proposition that can convince either of us. Is the universe love? Is that ridiculous? Try debating that!

7. This is alienating and unsettling. Am I positive about my views? What would it mean if you were right? What if I am 96% sure and 4% wobbly? Might that 4% so unnerve me that I lose my strength and maybe even my ability to function?

8. And imagine if this debate or disagreement is going on in one-and-the-same person? Two adamant, contradictory beliefs residing in the same brain. This regular happenstance gives us a beginning sense of the havoc wrought by the mystery divide.

9. This difference in core belief doesn't automatically cause two kirists to become enemies. But it is alienating and can play itself out in difficult and painful ways. The mystery divide separates secular folks from spiritual folks and can fracture the individual.

10. What do we even mean by that peculiar word, "mystery"? Is it meant to signify an actual feature of the world?

Are we talking about literal gods, literal psychic powers, literal spirits, literal astrological truths? Or are we talking about something else?

11. On the face of it, kirism doesn't seem like a philosophy of life that would much concern itself with mystery or grant mystery much of a place in human affairs. To a contemporary, science-loving rationalist, isn't "mystery" something of a dirty word?

12. It rather is. And yet, kirism must acknowledge the fact that for many people, and many kirists among them, "mystery" may be as important or more important than "reality." For those folks, a spiritual feeling may provide more information than a lecture.

13. Let's try to deconstruct the word. "Mystery" connotes various things. "Who killed the prince?" is one sort of mystery. "What happened before the big bang?" is another. "Did Christ walk on water?" is a third. In common parlance, these are all mysteries.

14. A first sense of mystery is "a puzzle to be solved." Who killed the prince? Was it his third wife? Was it the butler? Maybe the killer will be captured or maybe he or she or they won't. But there is nothing very startling or "mysterious" going on here.

15. There is just some current not knowing. Probably we will know at some point and the killer will be arrested. Or maybe this mystery will never be solved. Either way, kirists do not find anything particularly mysterious about mysteries of this sort.

16. A second sense of mystery is "a pseudo-puzzle to be solved." In this instance, there is no real puzzle, just an

ordinary something that happened. I thought I put my car keys down here. Oh, but look, they are way over there. How mysterious! No, not really.

17. Neither of these senses of "mystery" worry us or concern us very much. Who killed the prince? How did our car keys get over there? A philosophy of life can safely stay silent on the art of detection and on instances of everyday forgetfulness.

18. A third sense of mystery concerns things that look to be frankly unknowable—but unknowable in an obvious and trivial sense. We can't know if there were pancakes before the big bang or whether they came with syrup. Not a chance we can know that!

19. Such trivially unknowable "forever mysteries" also hardly trouble kirists, who find unknowable mysteries of that sort charmingly irrelevant. The rational mind knows exactly why such mysteries are unknowable and moves on to other things.

20. Puzzle mysteries, pseudo-puzzle mysteries, and trivially unknowable mysteries hardly threaten us, trouble us, or concern us much at all. They may be important to mystery writers and to astrophysicists but they don't agitate kirists.

21. What kirists do need, however, is a way of relating to those occurrences that make one wonder if we understand the universe at all. Apparent mysteries that cause us to wonder about and doubt the very nature of reality do concern us.

22. Such occurrences will matter to—and trouble—secular kirists and spiritual kirists differently. For the secular kirist, they may produce a fierce and distracting anger. For the

spiritual kirist, they may produce a fierce and distracting piety.

23. Let's make up a fanciful example and consider why we need a way of responding to it that serves our major goal of ethical life-purpose living. Here's something that at first glance seems pretty strange and unsettling. How might a secular kirist react?

24. You are strolling beside a lake. You see someone walking on water. Since you wonder if your eyes are perhaps playing tricks on you, you ask several people nearby if they also see that fellow walking on water. They vigorously assert that they do.

25. How might you respond to this odd occurrence? A spiritual kirist might be slightly inclined or even seriously inclined to embrace this occurrence as proof of the magical, the mystical, and the spiritual. A secular kirist is likely to respond differently.

26. A secular kirist's first thought might be, "Oh, he must be wearing hover boots of some sort. What interesting new technology! I've never seen that before." That lucky thought would end the matter with no harm done. On she'd stroll.

27. But what if you decide that this is a trick of some sort, some "walking on water" stunt? You suppose that if you cared enough, you'd be able to figure out how this stunt was pulled off; but you shake your head, signifying that you don't care.

28. Still, even though you may be able to shrug off what you presume is a stunt, you may well feel annoyed, agitated, even furious. Why are so many people always

trying to dupe other people? What will a child think who witnesses this nonsense?

29. How infuriating! Now, instead of considering what the next right thing to think might be, you find yourself fulminating against hucksters, tricksters, scam artists, and that whole wide world of devious folks whose default way of being is to deceive.

30. Your response might be even darker. It might be to presume that not only is this a trick or a stunt but that the people around you, the ones asserting that this young fellow is indeed walking on water, are in on the stunt, are all confederates.

31. It might cross your mind that this is some sort of experiment or manipulation aimed, for unknown and unknowable reasons, directly at you. This bit of paranoia is supremely unwelcome but also not fully unjustified, given the history of our species.

32. This particular line of thought is bound to raise your blood pressure. Whichever sort of agitated response you experience, it comes with a real cost. The cost might be bewilderment, dismay, anger, even fury. And one major cost is disruption.

33. This disruption will dramatically increase in magnitude if you are also a little bit seduced and confused by the occurrence. You see something that you can't easily explain and it might tempt you to doubt your very understanding of the universe.

34. You probably won't leap to a belief in reincarnation or heaven. This strange event doesn't really change your mind or fluster you that much. But it does angle you just a little

in the direction of "mystery" and may create an itch that can grow into a panic.

35. As a result of such sudden, subtle doubts, everything can seem fuzzier, hazier, and less solid. You discover that your ability to live intentionally and to meet your self-obligations has been harmed. All this over a strange occurrence at the lake!

36. This is a big result from what may indeed be a stunt pulled off as a simple practical joke, a joke on the order of teenage boys roaming around at night and creating "alien crop circles" that then produce a local panic. This silly stunt really got to you!

37. Likewise, a spiritual kirist may be subtly and powerfully affected. She may take this as further evidence that unseen forces animate the universe, making everything from classical science to common sense seem less reliable and impressive.

38. For her, this moment may affect her years later, when she is confronted by a cancer diagnosis and finds herself not knowing whether to trust traditional Western medicine, to go with an alternative spiritual approach, or to somehow marry the two.

39. It isn't that a spiritual kirist will fall to her knees reverentially. Rather, this odd moment may cause her to nod and deepen her reliance on mystery thinking—and maybe even while loud warning bells go off, chiming "Don't be too gullible here."

40. Like the secular kirist, she may find herself divided and agitated. On the one hand, she may believe in the miraculous and the mystical. On the other hand, she may half-

doubt her own belief system and question the wisdom of believing in unseen forces.

41. What to do? Both secular and spiritual kirists might first of all endeavor to handle this particular walking-on-water challenge by taking that kirist step to the side and creating a little space between the occurrence and some knee-jerk reaction.

42. A secular kirist might use that space to remind herself that it is her job to get and keep a grip on her mind and that she doesn't have to go down a rabbit hole of malaise over this occurrence. If she chooses, she can just smile a small smile and walk on by.

43. A spiritual kirist might use that space to remind herself that genuine mysteries are unlikely to present themselves in this commonplace way, any more than they are likely to present themselves as talking toads or magical tomatoes.

44. For this particular occurrence, a step to the side might prove adequate. No harm done to either the secular kirist or the spiritual kirist. But the mystery divide can play itself out in much more confusing and damaging ways.

45. Say that a secular kirist and a spiritual kirist marry. They agree on a lot, on almost everything. They share important values. They get along. They love one another. But the mystery divide is there, playing itself out in one or another of the following ways.

46. What if the person you live with and you love announces that he will only take homeopathic remedies for his chronic illness and that the elixir he swears by, which has absolutely no active ingredients, is pure magic? What then?

47. What if the person you live with and you love announces that a spell has been cast on her by a seriously unfriendly co-worker? Suddenly and immediately thereafter, she commences an actual, undeniable physical decline. What then?

48. What if the person you live with and you love wants to take your young son, who rarely speaks and who is showing all sorts of disturbing behaviors, to Tibet to spend a month with an energy healer specializing in autism? What then?

49. What if the person you live with and you love wants you to read a certain book channeled by another-worldly entity, a book that she enthuses is brilliant and powerful and that will change your outlook and your life? What then?

50. What if the person you live with and you love has decided to postpone starting his online business based on astrological considerations, even though you are 100% certain that right now is the best time to launch that business. What then?

51. What if the person you live with and you love bases her driving decisions on the numbers she sees on passing license plates, speeding up if she encounters certain numbers, slowing down if she encounters other numbers? What then?

52. What if the person you live with and you love informs you that she has just visited a traditional medicine woman who advised her to refuse all radiation and chemotherapy for her recently-diagnosed breast cancer? What then?

53. What if the person you live with and you love comes from a culture and a background where you are commanded to dip your newborn in a certain diphtheria-

infested river—and he intends to continue with that tradition? What then?

54. Now the mystery divide has come home to roost in ways that matter. If these were the sorts of disagreements where evidence would help settle them, that would be one thing. But they aren't. This is a divide that just can't be breached by evidence.

55. Both secular kirists and spiritual kirists have to come to grips with the alienating reality that with regard to psychic powers, homeopathic remedies, energy healers, acupuncture, aroma therapy, angel wisdom, and so on, agreement is impossible.

56. No one knows how to adequately handle the situation when two human beings have completely different views of how the universe is operating. The mystery divide is no joke, no mere annoyance, no mere inconvenience. It divides human beings.

57. The mystery divide really divides. Billions of human beings pay allegiance to mystery. Billions of human beings are antipathetic to mystery. Billions of human beings are confused as to what they really can and should believe and are internally divided.

58. What can be done? At a minimum, two kirists on either side of the mystery divide can decide to still love one another. They can smile. They can hug. They can kiss. Yes, one day some huge trench may open up out of the blue. But they can still love.

59. They can decide to still treat one another respectfully. As much as the one might want to convince the other, as much as the one might want to change the other's mind,

an attitude of respect can be maintained. This will be hard; but it is possible.

60. They can decide to still continue talking, even though each has made up his or her mind. Belief systems do change. Staunch opinions can shift. If you are still talking, that means that you have not arrived at a complete impasse.

61. And what if the divide is internal? What if you're essentially spiritual but worry that you're fooling yourself? What if you're essentially secular but worry that you're misunderstanding the universe? What can be done when the mystery divide is inside?

62. You are flying from San Francisco to Los Angeles tomorrow. Tonight, you have a vivid dream of the plane crashing. Do you shrug that off? Do you take it as a meaningful warning? What is either a secular kirist or a spiritual kirist to do with a premonition?

63. The rational mind has no answer, except to say, "That was nothing" or "That was anxiety." But it didn't feel like nothing and it didn't feel like anxiety. The mind is pulled and even obliged to presume that something non-ordinary just occurred.

64. Maybe nothing non-ordinary did just occur. Maybe it was just the way our anxiety about flying wanted to play itself out. But it is hard not to stew, hard not to toss and turn, and hard not to feel like something that ought to be heeded just happened.

65. And, if we are a secular kirist, that powerful feeling can shake our very belief system. If premonitions are real, what then? We spin out what that might mean and how

essentially wrong we may be about the workings of the universe.

66. Both the secular kirist and the spiritual kirist are likely to eventually shrug that feeling off and get on that plane. With only the rare exception, that is what we do. We dismiss or override that premonition and keep on living as usual.

67. But we get on that plane with extra trepidation, with our fingers more tightly crossed than usual, maybe even in a bit of a sweat. We don't like what we're feeling and we don't believe that we should be feeling that way, but we indubitably are.

68. This is the mystery divide pummeling the individual. Is it ridiculous to believe in premonitions? Is it ridiculous not to believe in premonitions? Why can't it all be clearer, exactly this or exactly that, and not some barbed-wire fence to ride?

69. Still, the occurrences come and the feelings come. We haven't spoken to a friend in ten years. We haven't thought about her in months. Today, we think about her. Ten minutes later we receive an email from her. Darn! What is that about?

70. Neither probability theory nor improbability theory are really convincing on this score. Yes, things that are a billion-to-one do happen. But, a billion-to-one? Really? And, besides, it didn't *feel* random. It felt very much like something else.

71. A spiritual kirist will likely smile at what feels like confirmation of mystery. At the same time, he may feel unsettled by the event. A secular kirist, shaking her head,

will definitely feel unsettled. Both will rather wish that email hadn't arrived.

72. Do we have to fight this odd occurrence off, so as to be true to some strict principle of no mystery ever? Or might such strictness freeze us and hurdle us toward meaninglessness? Or are there very good reasons for maintaining that strictness?

73. It might be nice to embrace that odd moment as a "who knows what" that maybe allows us to smile and to feel a bit of a sympathetic connection with what otherwise seems like an ice-cold universe. But isn't there a cost to that smile, too?

74. If we could just enjoy it, we might feel happier and somehow less down on the universe. Life might feel warmer by a degree or two and those few added degrees might prove the difference between despair and a lightness of being.

75. Maybe we don't have to fight that occurrence off as if "nothing happened" or insult our intelligence by acting as if a probabilistic explanation really makes sense. On the other hand, we can't quite just smile and enjoy it.

76. Maybe we have good reasons for being worried about smiling at that email and tacitly accepting the reality of non-ordinary events. That smile might just prefigure our own increased gullibility and irrationality. It just might open some door.

77. If we do not believe in made-up gods, then we do not want to let in those made-up gods by some back door. We do not want to suddenly freight words like "mystical" or "spiritual" or "metaphysical" with an importance in which we don't believe.

78. So, we can't quite smile. We know that the mystery divide has the power to separate parents and children, separate siblings, separate coworkers, and we wish it could just vanish. But while we wish for that outcome, we can't just smile the divide away.

79. A philosophy of life can't answer the question, "What's true?" It can't settle this mystery debate, close the mystery divide, or presume that an answer is waiting in the wings. Even the wisest philosophy of life has no power to do any of that.

80. It can, however, acknowledge the divide. It can exclaim, "Watch out!" And it can offer ideas about how secular kirists and spiritual kirists can lovingly coexist, even while an ontological Grand Canyon stands between them.

81. Of course, we want more than that. We want resolution, relief, assurances, comfort, a coming together. We want the truth and we want answers. We want the divide between us and within us to evaporate. And we can't have that.

82. We are each divided. We are built for rationality and also with an inclination, more in one person and less in another, to credit certain experiences and certain feelings as suggesting—and, for some, proving—the existence of an alternate reality.

83. Why is it important to look the mystery divide right in the eye? Because life requires that we make important choices, including life-and-death ones, and this divide makes arriving at those choices that much more difficult. It is a particular albatross.

84. Perhaps a bridge can be built that honors stalwart rationality and that likewise honors metaphysical possibili-

ties. Maybe there is some surprising missing link, more elusive than Darwin's, that can knit together the two halves of our species.

85. Or maybe that bridge can't be built. Maybe that divide is too great, too fundamental. Then we must return to our basic kirist practices and strive to live our life purposes, weighted down by these particular alienating differences in belief and outlook.

18

BOOK XVIII. HUMANISM AND THE SELFISH GENE

1. Kirists, like everyone, are born self-interested. They are born with selfish genes. But they do not love it that they are born that way, because they are also born with a conscience and a humanistic impulse. And so, a lifelong battle ensues.

2. They will want what they want. At the same time, they will find it crass that all human beings, themselves included, want what they want at the expense of morals and the greater good. This is a tension in every kirist, this mix of grandiosity and altruism.

3. The humanistic impulse is very strong in kirists. It is also very easy to define. It is that part of our nature that champions truth, beauty, and goodness. Kirists strive to embody the humanistic impulse, because they know it is their best self.

4. But they have other impulses as well. They want their slice of the pie. They want someone to say, "Well done!" They want to win the race, whatever that race may be.

They want the spoils of victory: the residency, the solo museum show, the Nobel Prize.

5. Maybe they keep this a secret from themselves. Maybe they say, "I don't need any of that. I don't need recognition. I don't need being paid. I don't need anyone knowing my name. I'm happy just to do my thing and be of service. I'm fine with that."

6. And then they find that they have no motivation, no desire, no energy. By beautifully reining in their selfish genes, they sadden themselves and secretly bristle. This bristling takes on its own energy and they grow critical, say, or despondent, or drink a lot.

7. Or they say a different thing. They say, "Sure, morals are all well and good. But I have to make my music! It's in my blood! Yes, I might do more good as a doctor treating the rural poor, but my music is so important to me—and, who knows, to the world!"

8. Or they make use of the way mystery can be invoked and announce, "I agree, it's not obvious how what I'm doing supports truth, beauty, and goodness, but I can feel how it does, in some inexplicable way that is completely real to me."

9. Or, having given life a thumb's down, they furiously assert, "Sure, I know all about truth, beauty, and goodness. But the world is such a damned unfair place and I've been treated so unjustly that I refuse to give a rat's ear about anybody's good!"

10. This all becomes so complicated in real life! The humanistic impulse gets knotted up with other impulses and produces weird, sometimes unfortunate, sometimes

tragic outcomes. It is so devilishly hard to maintain the purity of that impulse!

11. You are a medical researcher. You really want to find a cure for the disease you're researching. But when scientists on the other coast get to that cure first, you grow furious. They won! You forget all about the main point, that there is now a cure.

12. You are a choreographer. Your upcoming dance is brilliant, except for that tired middle bit. You could lift a wonderful sequence from that show you just saw, but that would be stealing. Or would it? Well, yes! But maybe no. Darn it!

13. You are a poet. Your family needs more money. There is no way you can contribute to the household kitty except by taking on some life-sucking job that will kill your creative soul. What will you do, defend your high status or toil away like a worker bee?

14. You are a great composer. You want to write a symphony in defense of freedom. That need is vibrating in your body. But the tyrant who runs your country is bound to retaliate and harm you and your family. Create? Or bow down and write pap?

15. You really want to write a cozy mystery series. But is light entertainment really of value? Is that how you're supposed to express the humanistic impulse, that trivially? You go back and forth, back and forth, and can't settle enough to write anything.

16. You run the philanthropic arm of a giant corporation. Your work is good and true. But you also know that your department is a public relations ploy meant to smooth over

the fact that your corporation is polluting mightily. Can you happily continue?

17. You're an architect with a thousand ideas. But is what you want to do just all ego and excess? Does the world really need your outlandish creations? Or does it need more affordable housing? How can you justify spending millions on the thrill of newness?

18. One minute you have the clear sense that truth, beauty and goodness matter—that nothing matters more. The next minute an impulse arises from some other place in your being, from some tricky place, some egotistical place, some angry place.

19. You see this dynamic already in little children. They are happily drawing. Then, when the carefree drawing ends, they suddenly and desperately need their drawing to be the one chosen to be pinned up. They are devastated if Johnny's or Mary's is chosen!

20. From smiles to tears, just like that. That is how it is with us. The smile of a desire to help, followed by the craven urge not to share our secrets. The smile of a beautiful idea, followed by the angry wonder as to whether anyone will applaud it or even care a little.

21. Truth, beauty, and goodness on the one side. Ego on the other. Pure love on the one side. Revenge fantasies on the other. A desire to serve on the one side. A desire to be applauded on the other. Selflessness on the one side. Selfishness on the other.

22. And even if your impulse remains pure, it must still butt up against the real world. You write an excellent screenplay. It is full of truth, beauty, and goodness. Then

nine studio writers get their hands on it and turn it into a bad joke version of your vision.

23. Our humanistic impulse wars with our other impulses and it also wars with the world. And it is devilishly hard to untangle, since words like truth, beauty, and goodness are themselves minefields. Plus, we have our formed personality to contend with.

24. One person grows up in one place, with one set of experiences, and the documentary film that flows out of his personality is a love poem to Palestinians. A second person grows up his way; and his documentary portrays Palestinians as the hated enemy.

25. Can both films be beautiful? Yes. Can both films be true? Yes. May both films represent the clear conscience of its creator? Yes. And kirists know this. They know that the humanistic impulse, filtered through a person, leads to results like these.

26. So, a kirist is pressured to wonder, is this whole truth, beauty, and goodness business a mirage, a trick of the mind, something that is really like quicksand for kirists? Is it a bad joke, another bit of absurdity? Do only idiots fall for that particular mind trick?

27. A kirist is forced to wonder, "How can an obscure poem ever be true, beautiful, and good when it is just some words on a page read by no one? Maybe it can be beautiful and true, but good? What good is it doing anyone, even the poet herself?"

28. She is forced to wonder, "Why not make a ton of money like some robber baron and then contribute to charity? Doesn't that actually help more people in the end

than toiling away at some moral job that makes no money and leaves me drained?"

29. And she would much rather not wonder in these ways. She would much rather not have all these contradictions, tensions, and absurdities to contend with. Her desire is to have the humanistic impulse make simple sense—but does it?

30. It is hard to see how it makes any simple sense. Look at the history of art. Art in the service of kings and queens and other tyrants, followed by urinals and cement dung, followed by splattering paint on canvas. Truth, beauty, and goodness? Really?

31. Is a urinal beautiful? And does sculpting a urinal come from the same place as sculpting a mother and her child, or a general, or a god, or an abstract cube, or a Confederate flag? Which of these are humanistic? Are they all? Really?

32. We stand confused. Is all art humanistic? If not, which is and which isn't? Is all music humanistic? If not, which is and which isn't? Is all self-expression humanistic? If not, which is and which isn't? Can anything sensible be said about such conundrums?

33. This confusion makes for misery. Is my scientific research meaningful or absurd? Is my movie a pleasant diversion or a ridiculous waste of a hundred million dollars? Is my political stand righteous or completely wrong-headed? Heavens!

34. Kirists would love this to be clearer. Wouldn't that be lovely, if we could say about this, "Ah, the humanistic impulse in action!", and about that, "Not so much." But

everything is so tangled, so subjective, so unclear, so uncertain.

35. And here come those selfish genes again! The self-serving humanitarian gesture. The wonder as to why I am pushing this: because it's worthy, because it's wanted, because it's sexy, because it's easy, because it feels good? Or all of that!

36. A nineteen-year-old is attending college. But he has no idea why he's there. He wants to be a rock drummer. That's all that he wants. He wants that life, those experiences, he wants to bang out rhythms as loud as he can.

37. Is this truth, beauty and goodness speaking? Or is it sex, drugs, and rock-and-roll? Or is it sex, drugs, and rock-and-roll with a few pinches of truth, beauty and goodness sprinkled in? He drops out of college, joins a band, and gets very drunk.

38. He does this for fifteen years. He has lots of experiences. He finds himself in many gutters. He plays many thrilling concerts. He loves the drumming, he loves the life, and he also hates the life, because he completely understands its dark underbelly.

39. At thirty-five he is forced to stop because his body is giving out. He also wants to stop, because he recognizes that he is not actually living his life purposes. He has been living the pulsating dream but now its nightmare side is just too apparent.

40. Was there any way to spare this would-be kirist those fifteen years? Was there any way for him to see that sex, drugs, and rock-and-roll was not the same thing as truth, beauty, and goodness? Or was that adventure inevitable and his destiny?

41. That is the macro. In the micro, every day we face this choice: humanism or the selfish gene? Something good for my brother or something good for me? Something beautiful to add to the world or some craven step to take? Every day we face this.

42. I clearly remember an incident from second grade. I'd been out sick for a few days and so had a classmate. When we got back, our teacher informed us that she'd handed out a new reader during our absence. She sent me to the book closet to get our copies.

43. In the closet were the two remaining readers, one in perfect condition and the other just a tiny bit shopworn. I knew what was coming. I was going to have to hand one to the girl and keep one for myself. What would I do?

44. I chose the better one for myself. I'm sure I had some excellent rationale for my choice. But I knew exactly what I was doing and exactly what I had done. I could therefore take no pleasure in having the better book, as I knew I had acted poorly.

45. Was this an earthshaking moment in the history of humankind? No. But it is telling that I remember it. Somewhere in your being you remember all those moments, too. You might have been generous but instead you were selfish. You know.

46. Of course, you had your reasons. Maybe they were excellent reasons, maybe they were reasons you saw right through yourself, maybe they were feelings masquerading as reasons, that driving impulse to drum drowning out everything else.

47. What is a kirist to do? Is he to say of the poem he just wrote "That satisfied my soul" or is he to say "What was

the point of that?" Is he to go on a spiritual journey to India when his neighborhood needs his talents, his muscles, and his heart?

48. Who is equal to teasing apart these contradictions and these warring impulses, the impulse for success, the impulse for sex, the impulse for generosity, the impulse for self-expression, the impulse to make one's mark? Am I? Are you?

49. And what will you actually do with the humanistic impulse? Say it manifests as the urge to create. Do you sit down and start a novel? Does that actually satisfy that urge? Or does it start you down the road of two years of difficulty, writing a hard-to-write novel?

50. Or, say, you're at the mall and witness a parent being cruel to his child. The humanistic impulse kicks in. But what can you do? Say something and risk a fistfight or a lawsuit? When you see a wrong and you want it to be right, what can you possibly do?

51. Or maybe it manifests as a love of architecture. What do you do? Spend a decade learning that profession, only to discover that you can't build what you want? Or do you do something much simpler, like take a tour of Italian architecture?

52. Or maybe it manifests as a powerful need to tell truth to power. But how do you tell a corporation the truth? March outside its headquarters until you're arrested? Send its CEO an email? Doesn't that stretch absurdity past the breaking point?

53. The humanistic impulse is not an itch that is that easy to scratch. Sometimes it can be satisfied by listening to a little Chopin. Too often it remains painfully

unquenched, just as does your urge to soar or to make everything right.

54. So, kirists are faced with the following. Our humanistic urge wars with our own selfish genes, it wars with the world, and it refuses to satisfy easily, even when our selfish genes don't get in the way. Doesn't that make it an eloquent burden?

55. It does. Still, it is our best nature speaking. Were we to find a way to rid ourselves of it, as by an appendectomy, who would we be? We would be a person we ourselves would not respect. Therefore, we need a plan.

56. We need a plan for supporting our humanistic impulse, a plan for discerning how to manifest it, a plan for keeping our selfish genes at bay, and a plan for dealing with a world indifferent or antagonistic to all our planning. A plan indeed!

57. Well, first we honor that impulse. We say "truth, beauty, and goodness" with a straight face, without a trace of irony or embarrassment. We understand what we are doing—opening a Pandora's box of difficulty—but we still say it.

58. And we make sure to mean it. We aren't just paying lip service to an ideal or to a charming notion. We say it with the same seriousness that we say "My loved one needs me." We say it the same way that we say, "I will live in a principled way."

59. We understand that the humanistic impulse is a poignant human burden. But we hold it not as a burden but as a beacon. We hold it as a beacon, as a touchstone, as a reverberation. We hold it as a pillar of hope, as a face of love.

60. Yes, it is demanding. We accept that reality. You have the impulse—then you accept the coming mountain of work. Do you think that novel will prove easy to write? That that cure is just around the corner? That righting that wrong requires just your pinky?

61. Your selfish genes may cry out, "I just want a feather bed! Some champagne, please! A ripe cheese! Not a year of frustration looking for a cure and not finding one. Comfort, please. Ease. Potato chips. A little golf. A few drinks at the club!"

62. Your selfish genes may cry out, "Everybody takes that shortcut! Why shouldn't I? Why shouldn't I be like the modal, the mean, and the median? Exactly average, ethically speaking, doing just enough, not caring very much, and fitting in perfectly?"

63. Your selfish genes may cry out, "Look, my coworker is so attractive. Isn't that the truth? Isn't that beautiful in its own way? Isn't intimacy a good thing? Yes, it would be a betrayal of my marriage, but, hey, isn't it true, beautiful, and good in its own way!"

64. Your selfish genes will whine, plead, cajole, trick you with language and metaphor, make you think that up is down and that down is up, and in every way a gene can play you aim you in the direction it wants, not where your best self wants to go.

65. Yes, the humanistic impulse is inconvenient and demanding. It is a real pressure. "Truth, beauty, and goodness" is not so sweet a refrain. Is the truth easy? Is beauty easy? Is goodness easy? The humanistic impulse is hardly a summer breeze!

66. We hold the humanistic impulse as a guiding beacon

while remembering how brilliantly our selfish genes can transform that pure impulse into something unworthy. Our genes can play us magnificently! Evolution has had a long time to work on it.

67. We remind ourselves not to say, "Ah, I am compelled to write that novel. The heck with everything else, my family included!" We remind ourselves not to say, as did Raskolnikov in *Crime and Punishment*, "Thievery is okay for an intellectual like me!"

68. We hope that, say, a beautiful symphony emerges out of us because that would be, well, beautiful. But we keep that symphony in clear context. If composing it amounts to too much selfishness, we admit that. We hate it; but we admit it.

69. Then we say, "What can be done?" By that we mean, "How can I have my symphony and also act honorably?" We sit with that question and try our best to arrive at a solution that honors both our humanistic impulse and our other self-obligations.

70. This becomes a core self-obligation: to cherish the humanistic impulse, to make sense of it, and to remain ethical. Maybe we make music that satisfies the soul; but we don't indulge in diva. We don't insult waiters just because our music is brilliant.

71. And what if the impulse vanishes? Well, we had better not let its disappearance go unnoticed. That it has vanished is a sign that something is not right in our world. It may, for instance, be a sign that we are despondent, sorrowful, or defeated.

72. Or it might mean that our circumstances are overwhelming us. The humanistic impulse can survive even in

concentration camps, where the victimized come together to form orchestras and play music, but circumstances can also kill it right off.

73. Or it might mean that we have grown too anxious and panicky. We can manifest the humanistic impulse while anxious, indeed we must, but when our anxiety becomes too high, then all we have, in mind and in body, is an overwhelming sense of danger.

74. Or it might mean that some new avenue for its expression is needed. The old roads may feel tired and shopworn. Maybe we suffered too many defeats and failures. Maybe we are grieving what we have lost and find ourselves between expressions.

75. Truth, beauty, and goodness. This is certainly not the only way to describe the humanistic impulse. We would want to include other ideas, about freedom, about self-expression, about the heart, about compassion, about improving and saving our world.

76. Still, truth, beauty, and goodness is reasonable shorthand. It is easy to remember and close to the mark. But it does lead to one conundrum: should beauty really be included? Should beauty be put on the same pedestal as truth and goodness?

77. We understand without hesitation the virtues of truth and goodness. Beauty is an odder duck. Where is the virtue in a fire that is burning down a building, even if it rapturous to watch? What is there to honor or applaud in that beautiful sight?

78. The Russian novelist Alexandr Solzhenitsyn meditates in his Nobel Prize acceptance speech on his countryman's Fyodor Dostoevski's remark, "Beauty will save the world."

Solzhenitsyn is skeptical about that sentiment, as we all should be.

79. Solzhenitsyn writes: "For a long time, I considered it mere words. How could that be possible? When in blood-thirsty history did beauty ever save anyone from anything? Ennobled, uplifted, yes – but whom has it saved?" He is obliged to shake his head.

80. Still, he considers the matter; and concludes that in those times when truth and goodness were crushed, as they were during the regime of Stalin, beauty helped hope survive. He concludes that beauty does have a legitimate place alongside truth and goodness.

81. He writes: "So perhaps that ancient trinity of Truth, Goodness and Beauty is not simply an empty, faded formula? In that case Dostoevsky's remark, 'Beauty will save the world,' was not a careless phrase but a prophecy." It may be prophetic still.

82. Yes, the three must go together: beauty alone is too suspect and will not do. But when they do march hand-in-hand, when truth, beauty and goodness unite, then beauty helps truth and goodness reach, open, and finally warm the human heart.

83. I hope that kirism is that sort of thing: true, beautiful, and good. Of course, I can have only an imperfect understanding of whether or not I've succeeded and whether or not my selfish genes have intruded too terribly. I can't know for sure.

84. Kirists nod. They recognize that they have only an imperfect understanding of the many traps that make manifesting their humanist impulse so difficult, traps set by

their selfish genes, traps set by the world, traps set by the humanistic impulse itself.

85. But they do not waver. They do not relegate "truth, beauty and goodness" to the dust heap of nineteenth century idealism. It remains alive in them, mixed up with a hundred other impulses but not just as one among many: it is first among those many.

19

BOOK XIX. KIRIST PRACTICES

1. There are no prescribed kirist practices. It would be lovely if kirists paid attention to their life purposes, engaged in absurd rebellion, asserted their individuality, did the next right thing, and so on. But we have no prescribed "ways" of doing any of that.

2. There are no particular things that you are obliged to do at 4 a.m., 2 p.m. or 10 p.m. You do not need to turn east, west, north or south. You do not need to come together or stay apart. That is between you and you or between you and other kirists.

3. But while there are no prescribed things to do, there are many wise things to do. Living as a kirist means putting kirism into practice, whether with around-the-clock practices, like doing the next right thing, with daily practices, or with intermittent practices.

4. What follows are thirty possible kirist practices. None are obligatory. All make sense. Try some out, if you like. If one serves you, keep it. If it doesn't, discard it. Who knows: it

may serve you later, in a year or two, when you find yourself in a different situation.

5. Practice 1. You might work on your kirist vocabulary, as if you were studying a new language. You might insert phrases like "absurd rebellion," "self-obligation," "meaning opportunities" and "meaning investments" into your internal conversations.

6. Pick some kirist word or phrase from the books of kirism. Maybe it's a rich word like "individual." Maybe it's the rich idea of "multiple life purpose choices." Chew on that word or phrase. Explore it. Say it out loud, maybe often. Live it.

7. Practice 2. You might start each day with a life purpose check-in. This might be quite a formal practice where you sit yourself down, remind yourself of your current life purpose choices, and mindfully select the ones you intend to champion that day.

8. Or it might be a simple stretch, yawn, and wonder: "What are my life purpose efforts for today?" Wouldn't that simple wonder point you in a better direction than if you rose and began stewing about the items on your irreducible to-do list?

9. Practice 3. You might practice doing the next right thing. To begin with, you might need to have a conversation with yourself about what the phrase "do the next right thing" signifies to you. This rich, subtle phrase requires your personal understanding.

10. The next right thing might be an ethical thing. The next right thing might be a necessary thing. The next right thing might be an appropriate thing. The next right thing might be a desirable thing. Can't

these all be right? They can! So, you will need to choose.

11. Doing the next right thing is an art form, not a slogan. It is a big, wonderful, humane intention, in conflict with our selfish genes and our rapacious appetites, exactly what we know to do, and exactly what is so hard to do. It is certainly worth a practice!

12. Practice 4. You might inaugurate and maintain a daily morning practice in the service of your life purposes. This might be a creativity practice, a health practice, a career-building practice, a mindfulness practice, a personality upgrade practice, and so on.

13. You would wake up and go directly to your practice. You would engage with it for fifteen minutes, for two hours, or however long. This would amount to a daily meaning investment and a daily meaning opportunity and might lead to the daily experience of meaning.

14. How about that for a kirist practice, one that offers you the possibility of meaning and the opportunity for meaning on a daily basis! Maybe you'll decide on multiple daily practices, providing you with multiple daily meaning opportunities.

15. Practice 5. You might redesign your mind. It is a kirist conceit, one, however, that is based in reality, that we can get a better grip on our mind than is usually supposed. We can shoot for the high-bar goal of only thinking thoughts that actually serve us.

16. More than that, we can employ the kirist concept of indwelling and decide to indwell in a different, better way, in, for instance, a calmer way or a more focused way, so

that the experience of "living in the room that is our mind" is altogether finer.

17. This would be a practice, then, of banishing thoughts that don't serve you and thinking thoughts that do serve you; and at the same time redesigning your mind, for instance by adding windows that let in a welcome breeze.

18. Practice 6. You might practice energy management and energy wisdom. What might that look like? Well, you might begin by making a two-column list of activities and habits that drain your energy and activities and habits that increase your energy.

19. Kirists understand that energy is a particularly mysterious component of the human story, neither easy to grasp nor easy to manage. But that makes energy management all the more magnificent a practice, a cross between wisdom and wizardry!

20. Practice 7. You might practice giving life a thumbs-up. We could each of us produce a million reasons why life does not deserve that affirmative gesture. But it nevertheless requires it, if we are to live with hope and efficacy and if we are to hold up the world.

21. What might such a practice look like? It might look exactly as it sounds: several times a day, you might say to yourself, "I'm now taking a moment to give life a hearty thumbs-up." You would turn in the direction of life and give it that thumbs-up gesture.

22. Or you might do something less literal. You might identify your most life-affirming life purpose and give it top priority. Or you might reframe "thumbs-up" as "love" and lavish some love on a person, a cause, or a creative project.

23. Practice 8. You might pick a windmill with which to joust. A feature of the kirist principle of absurd rebellion is identifying a worthy cause and galloping off to right that wrong. It is not enough to just notice an injustice: we must then hop right on our mule.

24. Or maybe we don't reach for our lance. Maybe our practice of absurd rebellion looks different from that. Maybe it has more to do with whimsy and gentle irony or maybe it is more a practice of small gestures and barely perceptible revolts.

25. Practice 9. You might create a formal practice of world discernment, a regular practice where you step back and wonder how you are being held in sway by your group, your religion, your television tastes, your work culture.

26. How might this work? Maybe every Wednesday at seven p.m. you would sit down with your notebook, blink several times to free yourself from the cultural trance, and ask yourself the question, "What's going on in my world that I should be aware of?"

27. You would hold yourself open to answers and, if some answer demanded that you take action, you would leap right up and act. Maybe you would resign some membership, drop some subscription, or put up storm windows against the impending storm.

28. Practice 10. You might turn the metaphor of available personality into an actual practice. Maybe you see yourself behaving in a way that doesn't please you. You whisper, "Ah, formed personality! Let me see what resources I have available."

29. You would then take an available personality resource inventory or in some other fanciful way play with the idea

that of course you feel stuck, as that is exactly what having a formed personality means, but that you are also genuinely free.

30. You might go a step further and do some real thinking about the relationships among original personality, formed personality and available personality as those ideas apply to you. That would likely prove an excellent, eye-opening practice!

31. Practice 11. You might practice taking direct aim at your greatest life purpose challenge or meaning challenge. Maybe it's your meaningless job. Maybe it's the rough ride of sobriety. Maybe it's your anger, your indifference, or your despair. Aim there!

32. Aim how? Well, you might work in a daily way to align your thoughts and your behaviors with your intention. Is it your intention to leave your current job and create that non-profit you've always dreamed of starting? Then think it and do it.

33. You would think "I am leaving my meaningless job and I am starting my non-profit." Then you might make two lists, the leaving list and the starting list. Then you might do one thing from each list. What a useful meeting-my-challenges practice!

34. Practice 12. You might practice personality preparation. You have a business meeting coming up in a few minutes. Who do you want to be? That caustic, arrogant fellow you have in you? That too-meek fellow? Or someone kinder and stronger?

35. This could become a kind of instantaneous check-in where you remind yourself in the blink of an eye of how you want to employ your available personality: say, during

your lunch hour, while you're helping Johnny with his homework, or when it's raining hard.

36. Practice 13. You might practice filling free time with purpose. Those two hours in the evening when you have "nothing to do" and can do "whatever you want" could be treated as carefully and as seriously as any other two hours of your life.

37. You might use those two hours to practice calmness. You might fill them with pent-up curiosity. You might relax so deeply that you actually relax. "Free time" can be difficult time spent right at the edge of the void: you might practice filling it with right intention.

38. Practice 14. You might practice handling meaning crises more effectively. One moment life feels meaningful, then something happens, and suddenly the meaning is gone. Intellectually, you may know what happened. But emotionally, you may not be prepared at all.

39. You run into your brother, who reminds you that you are poor and that you will always be poor, like every other poet. Plus, your poetry is inscrutable and pretty ridiculous. Plus, you broke your mother's heart by becoming a poet. And so on.

40. You try not to let his words affect you. You know that he hates his job and his life. But you also know that you just received a painful blow in the solar plexus of meaning. Practice may help! Practice may help prevent you from doubling over.

41. What sort of practice? To begin with, the simple practice of reminding yourself, maybe in a daily way, that blows to meaning happen all the time, that meaning is that sort

of thing; and that meaning is also a wellspring and an infinite resource.

42. Yes, something may knock the wind out of meaning. But the only thing that happened is that you had an experience. A bad one, yes, but just an experience. By this very evening meaning may return, all dusted off, and there you will be, ready to write your next sonnet.

43. Practice 15. You might design and fabricate a life purpose icon. Picture a simple piece of jewelry, so rich in its imagery and its resonance that every time you touch it you know exactly why to live and exactly how to live. A charm on a bracelet can do that!

44. Stop and imagine that icon. A bolt of lightning? A sturdy oak? An eagle in flight? A musical note? An exclamation point? Entwined lovers? What will yours be? Something small and precious or something monumental and impossible to ignore?

45. Practice 16. You might craft a life purpose statement. Such a statement can't do complete justice to all of a kirist's desires, purposes, and obligations, but it just might serve as a bit of a perfect reminder, exactly the way "Do the next right thing" does.

46. Your practice might be to craft your life purpose statement and then to recite it nine times a day, or whenever you feel bereft of meaning, or whenever the idea of absurd rebellion strikes you as too absurd, or maybe just once a day, first thing each morning.

47. Practice 17. You might practice a ceremonial bridging of the mystery divide. Maybe every third evening you'll visit a spot where the night sky is visible and do two things

at once: nod to astronomy and feel trembling awe, giving each its exact due.

48. Maybe as a residue of that experience you'll hand-build star-studded black pottery, bridging the divide that way, or tell your grandchildren stories about the meteor people who visit every hundred years, or just wear a silly grin as you think about saving the galaxy.

49. Practice 18. You might practice surrendering to not knowing. Such a practice would help you calmly tolerate all that is not known and can never be known. You might begin to softly murmur "I just don't know about that," rather than exclaiming that in horror.

50. You might create a ceremony of surrender to not knowing, bowing daily in the direction of mystery or nodding wisely at the inexplicable. Or you might create a mantra that you intone twice a day: "I know enough to navigate this life."

51. Practice 19. You might practice choosing love as a meaning opportunity. All that would take is a softening of the heart and an object of affection. If you bestow love today, you might also coax some meaning into existence. And you could do that again tomorrow.

52. Think of words in the family of love: affection, kindness, generosity, intimacy. They paint a picture of what loving looks like. Today, you might invest some meaning in loving a friend, in loving a cause, or in loving a symphony waiting to be written.

53. Practice 20. You might practice good works as a meaning opportunity, picking principled works that embody your values. In the Army, during one Korean

monsoon season, it was filling sandbags to save the surrounding villages from flooding.

54. Nothing elegant. Nothing arcane. Just filling sandbags, cleaning toilets at the shelter, keeping an eye on the neighborhood children. Mundane good works are hardly mundane if they match our values and if they produce the experience of meaning.

55. Practice 21. You might practice leading. Kirists are leaders sometimes by choice but always by obligation. They are obliged to lead because ethical living demands it. Your culture says one thing but you know another thing to be true: and so, you must lead.

56. Maybe you'll lead only reluctantly. Maybe you'll lead while full of worry and completely at sea. Maybe you'll take two giant steps forward and seven small steps back. This is surely worthy of practice, this sometimes-queasy leadership of the adamant kirist.

57. Practice 22. You might practice excellence. As children, we start out with two energies, both of which quite appeal to us: we love to experiment and we love to excel. Soon, though, life's hard lessons can cost us our taste for each.

58. Because we're pressured to get things right, we start to lose our taste for experimentation. And because much of what we do doesn't rise to the level of excellence, we begin to fear that excellence isn't in us. Both can drop by the wayside.

59. So, you might remind yourself to practice daily excellence, fully aware that excellence is a rare commodity, fully aware that eighty-six percent of life is ordinary, fully aware that aiming for excellence in no way guarantees it. But what a worthy goal!

60. Likewise, you might experiment. Let's call that practice 23, the practice of heroic messes, the practice of I-have-no-idea, the practice of seeing if blue and red make purple or if they make mud. Who knows, maybe you'll land on a whizzbang to patent!

61. Or maybe you'll land on something beautiful. Or maybe you'll land on a huge pile of manure. Experiments can lead to great successes but they regularly do so only by way of countless detours, potholes, and cliffhangers.

62. Put the act of experimentation and the possibility of excellence together and you get creativity. Let's call that practice 24. The practice of creativity can mean writing a novel, daydreaming in technicolor, or ingeniously outflanking your enemy.

63. Creativity is that rich, large word that stands for the way that we can make real use of our talents and inner resources. It is an activity, a method, a process, an attitude, a beneficence, a challenge, a way of being, all rolled up together.

64. A potentially creative person is not a creative person. Creativity is a manifestation. That makes it a perfect kirist practice, the alchemical practice of turning potentiality into, on some days, a complete mess, and on other days, a bit of a masterpiece.

65. Practice 25. You might try relating to others. Kirists first of all protect their individuality. Protecting our individuality requires that we remain separate, think our own thoughts, dream our own dreams, and stay in our own skins. But there is more to life than that!

66. While solitude is precious, relationships can prove heart-warming, golden meaning opportunities. They are

the place to love and be loved; the place to befriend and be befriended; the place to be human in the company of other human beings.

67. Envision your practice of warmer relating, of more mutuality, of richer closeness. What does it look like? You and a friend watching a movie? A long chat with your sister punctuated by raucous laughter? Something very grand or something homey and miniature?

68. Practice 26. You might practice stewardship. Stewardship is a combination of activism and compassion, a stance and a way of being that announces that you are willing to steer the ship, light the way, and put the world on your broad or narrow back.

69. Evolution has built the primacy of survival right into us. But it has also provided us with a sense of right and wrong and an understanding of ideas like mutuality and shared humanity. It has generously provided us with a word like stewardship.

70. We can aim ourselves in the direction of care for the world in which we live, for the creatures of this world, and for the ideas and institutions that maintain civilization at its best. We can steward our children; we can steward the nation.

71. Practice 27. Life will bring us sorrows but it can also provide us with joys and pleasures—the more so if we make it a regular practice to believe in pleasure, to be open to pleasure, and to accept the pleasures that life can offer.

72. Because of familial, cultural, and religious injunctions against enjoying pleasure, or because we think that pleasure is too low a thing to honor, we often summarily reject

it. What an odd and unfortunate idea! How could practicing joy not benefit us?

73. Practice 28. One of the consequences of the kirist demand of self-obligation is that we know that we ought to be activists. We understand the abiding connection between self-obligation and activism. This is an obvious—but hard—kirist practice.

74. Kirists may well not love it that they are obliged to hold up the world. But they may still choose to do exactly that. Donning the uniform of the absurd rebel—those tattered jeans, that funny hat—they commit to whole-hearted, reluctant activism.

75. Practice 29. You might practice taking better care of yourself. Stress is a reality, overwhelm is a reality, chronic illness is a reality, pressures on the mind and pressures on the body are realities. What sort of sense would it make for a kirist to ignore any of that?

76. Self-care is a self-obligation that cries out to be turned into multiple daily practices: the daily practice of enough sleep, the daily practice of friendly self-talk, the daily practice of loving self-kindness, the daily practice of a nice, brisk walk.

77. Practice 30. You might strive for and work toward personhood, integrating kirist ideas about indwelling, personality, ethics, life purposes, and meaning-making into a felt ground of being, with the world solid beneath your feet.

78. You would step out each day as yourself, facing the reality of the world, confronting the hard edges of your own personality, sighing at the enormity of your self-oblig-

ations, and heroically, solemnly, and maybe even joyfully living your life purposes.

79. There is power in the idea of practice. The very idea of practice can become a kirist practice. What could better support your intention to live life exactly as you intend to live it than creating and maintaining real life purpose-driven daily practices?

80. Think of all of the possibilities: a creativity practice, a health practice, a mindfulness practice, a relationship practice, a stewardship practice, a warrior practice. Wouldn't that amount to a rather excellent life?

81. The wisdom of these thirty practices is likely self-evident. Even so, they are not commandments. If they strike you as self-obligations, then and only then are you obliged to adopt them. If some or even many of them ring no bell, let them pass right on by.

82. You might enjoy saying, "I love the idea of kirist practices. I think I'll create a nice assortment of them!" Then you might create that assortment or collection, which might include some of the above and also many of your own.

83. If your collection grows enormous, what then? You may have to pick a few as your top three or your top five and hold tight to those. A few practices really embraced and fully lived is a better outcome than a monumental list that gathers dust in a corner.

84. Live your practices. If they try to slip out the door, chase them with a net. If they try to fall off the table, leap to their rescue. As a kirist, you've already set the bar high. Maintain it at that eloquent height by identifying and living your kirist practices.

85. There are no prescribed kirist practices and there is no dictatorship of practice. But there are plenty of logical, lovely practices that one could recommend whole-heartedly. There are really so many fine things that a kirist might try!

20

BOOK XX. ANALECTS OF KIRISM

1. Analects are ideas, sayings, phrases or fragments of a philosophy. The most famous are the Analects of Confucius, attributed to Confucius and believed to have been written and compiled by his followers. Here are some analects of kirism.

2. If a philosophy of life makes sense to you, then it has great value. But first of all, it ought to make sense to you. Your only reasonable criterion for embracing a philosophy of life is that it matches your understanding of life. Other criteria are humbug.

3. If angels and devils make no sense to you, if a dogmatic path to nirvana comprised of exactly seven steps makes no sense to you, if multiple gods each with an ax to grind make no sense to you, then neither ought a philosophy of life based on them.

4. You could try to tease out the acceptable bits of each such philosophy, arguing that the wheat is worth the chaff, but you won't feel convinced or satisfied. For a philosophy

of life to feel worth adopting, its essentials had better make sense to you.

5. What ought a contemporary philosophy of life include? It should speak to loneliness, emptiness, the drudgery of work, the challenges of identifying life purposes and maintaining meaning, and everything else genuinely important to you.

6. It ought to include our current understanding that we are at the brink of extinction, that the threats facing human beings are unlike any faced before in the history of the species, and that this tragic understanding is our truth and our burden.

7. It should not include any gods or other supernatural authorities bossing you around. They do not exist and you can be frankly done with them. That little pang of loss is nothing compared to the great joy (and, yes, sorrow) of freedom and self-authorship.

8. The payoff shouldn't be elsewhere, in another life. This is your one life. You can daydream about heavens, you can pine for celestial meet-ups with old friends and heroic ancestors, but you have this singular life to live, fully and for the good of all.

9. It ought to be psychologically-minded and take into account human nature. If it acts like human beings do not go to war for petty reasons, do not hate as much as they love, do not fail to meet their obligations, and all the rest, skip it as unbelievable.

10. It should have a way of speaking about personality that makes sense to you. It should help you understand the difference between original personality and formed person-

ality and what a likely much-needed personality upgrade might look like.

11. It should have a way of speaking about meaning that makes sense to you. It should make a clear distinction between the folly of seeking meaning and the genuine possibility of coaxing enough meaning into existence to allow life to feel meaningful.

12. It should have a way of speaking about life purpose that makes sense to you. It should make a clear distinction between the misleading idea of "a purpose to life" and replace that with the updated idea of multiple life purposes that you yourself choose.

13. It should have a way of speaking about ethics that makes sense to you. It should do a strong job of balancing two truths, that ethical action is as simple as doing the next right thing and also profoundly difficult, because life is complex and ambiguous.

14. It should have a way of speaking smartly about our dual nature as an individual and a social animal. It should remind us that in social situations, from cocktail parties to political rallies, we may be a version of ourselves that we neither recognize nor admire.

15. It should have a way of speaking smartly about our dual nature as selfish and selfless. Philosophies that do not take into account the reality of genetic selfishness must founder, as they presume us to be more loving and charitable than we are.

16. It should take into account our lived experience of trauma, love, pain, happiness, and all the rest. Human beings have experiences that matter. A philosophy of life

mustn't ignore the power of experience to shape our thinking, feeling and acting.

17. It should not close the door on mystery. It should first of all consider a creaking door to be about rusty hinges and not ghosts and it should for the most part let science arbitrate and explain. But it should also possess a little sympathy for mystery.

18. It should be for rationalism, science, and the scientific method. It should at the same time predict that billions of our species will hate rationalism, science and the scientific method, prefer superstition and ignorance, and fiercely attack rationalists.

19. It should point out the enormous divide between people like you and people not like you. A freedom-fighting folksinger will never see eye-to-eye with an authoritarian cleric or the dictator who supports him—or be safe from either of them.

20. It should have a lot to say about the ways in which how we think affects who we are and how we live. It should make a simple, smart and useful distinction between thinking thoughts that serve us and thinking thoughts that thwart us and harm us.

21. A philosophy of life ought to make sense to you and have you nodding in agreement because it strikes you as consistent, coherent, and lifelike. It should make sense to you from beginning to end and not just here and there or in its best bits.

22. Kirists believe that our species evolved. The universe did not plan for us and nothing supernatural cares about us. It might be comforting to think otherwise but there are

no gods looking out for us and no watchmakers, blind or otherwise, who created us.

23. Our species evolved to include consciousness. We have a consciousness of good and evil, a consciousness of our own mortality, and a consciousness of ourselves as contradictory creatures. Consciousness is our talent and our albatross.

24. We have a relationship with our own consciousness that in kirism we call in-dwelling. We dwell within, thinking, musing, telling stories, plotting our revenge, and all the rest. There, and not in the so-to-speak real world, is where we primarily live.

25. How we in-dwell determines how we live. If it is chaotic in there, we live chaotically. If we are raging in there, we live enraged. If we muffle our own thoughts, we live in a sad, muffled way. Your style of in-dwelling is the truth about you.

26. It is tense and intense inside of us. Our experience of in-dwelling is not like a walk in the park. We obsess, race along, worry, fret, pine, desire, confuse ourselves, and try to make sense of, and deal with, our radically contradictory impulses.

27. Our species evolved with contradictory impulses. We can be humane or cruel, charitable or greedy, careful or impulsive, clear-eyed or deluded, brave or timid, loving or hateful, all in the very same person, and even all on the very same day.

28. That is who we are. We are a member of a particular species. A lion cub is born a lion, a baby seal is born a seal, and we are born human. Like it or not, we are this particular sort of creature and not some other sort of creature.

29. We are born already somebody. We are born with built-in instructions, built-in differences, built-in proclivities, built-in needs, built-in desires, and a coherent but unknowable original personality. We are idiosyncratically ourselves from birth.

30. That we are born already somebody has grave import and huge consequences. What will it be like for you if you are twice as smart or half as smart as other human beings? What will it be like for you if you are born sensitive, stubborn or sad?

31. A philosophy of life must acknowledge the extent to which you must deal with the reality of life, including the reality of you. Right from the beginning you are a particular member of a particular species, with all that suggests, demands and entails.

32. Right from the beginning we are obsessive. Watch how a child needs his toys to be lined up just so. See the explosive tantrum that ensues if you knock one of his toys off its mark. This obsessiveness is not a disorder but a feature of our nature.

33. Right from the beginning we are destructive. Watch how a child gleefully knocks down the thing she has just built with at least as much energy as she built it. Indeed, doesn't she often build it just so as to knock it down? We are wired to be destructive.

34. Right from the beginning we are creative. Every child wants to draw silly giraffes. Every child wants to dance like a dervish. Every child wants to sing along at music time. Every child wants to listen to stories and make up stories. We are wired to create.

35. Right from the beginning we tell ourselves stories. A

child may begin to fantasize about how his real parents will come and rescue him from these mean parents who are making his life miserable. He may tell himself this story over and over again.

36. Telling stories becomes a lifelong habit, blessing, and trap. We tell ourselves stories that amuse us, motivate us, and cheer us. We also tell ourselves stories that demoralize us, that mislead us, and that send us on some very wild misadventures.

37. Kirists grow wise about the beauty and power of story-telling, on the one side, and the dangers and shadow side of story-telling, on the other. We understand the seductive nature of language and of narrative and are careful not to be seduced.

38. Right from the beginning, we sense our dual nature as fair-minded and selfish. We know that it is right to share that toy and we know that we do not want to share that toy. Maybe we share it and maybe we bite our playmate who tries to take it.

39. Right from the beginning, we sense this tension between sharing and biting. This tension may never go away, looking like a fight between playmates at age three, a fight between lovers at age twenty, and a fight between companies at age forty.

40. Likewise, we sense our need to compete and our desire for mastery. We prefer to win rather than to lose, to be picked first for the team rather than last, and to have our drawing put up on the classroom wall rather than be rejected by our teacher.

41. We may be trained to assert that "everyone is a winner," even those who finish last, and that "trying your

best" is as good as actual mastery. But it's unlikely that those homilies will ever ring quite true. Who really likes error-filled piano recitals?

42. At the same time, we sense that we have something in us that is worth something, something in us that wants to be explored, something in us that wants to ring out. This has been called our human potential, as in "the human potential movement."

43. We may be taught to be modest or beaten into not speaking and this may curtail our ability to manifest our potential. But we will know that we are falling short of what may have been possible. We will feel that disappointment and that despair.

44. We may therefore end up with a lifelong dynamic of starting things, because of all that felt potential, and then dropping them precipitously, out of anxiety, fear, doubt, shame, a lack of self-confidence, or an inability to tolerate the rigors of process.

45. Kirists understand that they must take charge in this regard, even if they have been subdued by society or harmed by their family, and honor their competitive desires, their craving for mastery, and their need to manifest their human potential.

46. To sum up these needs, we crave success. We also want success to be on our own terms, not as it appears to others or to the world. A poet may climb the ladder at the bank where she works, but what if her poems are never published?

47. She may not feel successful, even as she wins awards and garners pay raises. A significant amount of the despair that we feel connects to our felt lack of success in those

areas that matter the most to us. A lack of success is demoralizing.

48. We struggle. We struggle to succeed and often don't feel equal to that struggle. We struggle to make sense of our situation and to know what to do next. We struggle to balance what we want with what we know is right. We recognize that life is a struggle.

49. Right from the beginning we struggle to be ourselves and to manifest ourselves. This struggle plays itself out in all sorts of ways, from a restless conformity that leads to secret vices to a reckless individuality that leads to agitation and confrontations.

50. We look around us and we find ourselves obliged to deal with others of our species. But what should we make of what we see? We see behaviors, not the insides of people. And we are rather quick to label those behaviors as one thing or another.

51. What does it really mean to be human? Every vested interest specialist, from cleric to psychiatrist, from sociologist to judge, paints one sort of narrow, unconvincing picture. We reject their self-serving characterizations and try to decide for ourselves.

52. Watch a two-year-old rush from digging in the sand box to chasing a bird to climbing on the monkey bars. Is this a genuine shifting of interest, the thing nowadays called "hyperactivity," or a preview of an incipient, lifelong meaning problem?

53. As kirists, we are slow to label. We do not find that words and phrases like "depression" or "obsessive-compulsive disorder" or "attention deficit hyperactivity disorder"

explain enough, tell the truth, or do much more than falsely and conveniently label.

54. We observe our species and build our philosophy of life from what we see and from our speculations about what those observations signify, being careful to remember the extent to which circumstances, especially circumstances of birth, matter.

55. Metaphorically, a penthouse may be a prison. But a penthouse is not a prison and a prison is not a penthouse. Circumstances matter. If you are born into a society that worships alligators and that engages in ritual sacrifices, that seriously matters.

56. We are dropped into the circumstances of our birth. More and more circumstances occur and our original personality starts to transform itself into our formed personality, that too-inflexible, too-reactive everyday way of being that people know us by.

57. That formed personality, with its whispers of its original nature, with its remaining freedom, with its particular in-dwelling style, with its contradictions, peeves and obsessions, is the primary thing that we must deal with, daily and throughout our lifespan.

58. We deal rather poorly and contribute to our unwanted states. We do not ask for outcomes with names like depression, mania, obsessive-compulsive disorder, attention deficit disorder, and the like, but nevertheless we inadvertently contribute to them.

59. So much feels contradictory! We love this about life and we hate that. We have reasons for doing the work we do and are bored to tears by the work we do. We would

love to share but we still feel like biting. Who should we be? What should we do?

60. Bombarded by contradictory thoughts and feelings, we stand confused. Kirism acknowledges the inevitability of such confusion. We do not say, "How stupid of us to be confused!" We say, "How human of us to have to endure contradictions!"

61. What sorts of contradictions? You're thrilled by a march and feel patriotic. Then you hate yourself for your susceptibility to flag-waving. You stand confused, believing that patriotism is a home for rascals but also feeling love for the Constitution.

62. What sorts of contradictions? You're lonely and crave company. But you also rather prefer your own company to the company of others. You stand confused, wanting to be social, needing something from others, but not liking people all that much.

63. What sorts of contradictions? We start out idealistic and we also start out selfish. Ideally, we might prefer not to harm any other living creature. But we want that pastrami sandwich. Do we opt for severe principle or do we reach for the mustard?

64. What sorts of contradictions? We'd love not to be so buffeted by our experiences. But we are psychological creatures, not automatons, and therefore criticism hurts, humiliation hurts, loss hurts, even as we wish that we could live above the fray.

65. What sorts of contradictions? We have an excellent brain capable of all sorts of wonders. But it also presents us with nightmares, feelings we can't shake, and unhappy

thoughts that keep rattling tirelessly. What contrary gray matter!

66. What sorts of contradictions? That on some days your interests interest you and that on other days they do not. That on some days your loved ones fill you up and that on other days they deplete you. That the experience of things is annoyingly shifty.

67. What sorts of contradictions? That we love eloquence and know that we can be seduced by it. That we love beauty and know that we can be seduced by it. That we love the truth but wonder what "the truth" means any more—or ever meant.

68. What sorts of contradictions? You'd love to embrace humanity. You also know that you must defend yourself against humanity. One day you volunteer in a food kitchen and the next day you build a higher fence between you and your neighbors.

69. What sorts of contradictions? You'd like political candidates to be judged on their merits. But you're aware that in every important election, the taller candidate usually wins. What is civilization to do when it is running on archaic principles?

70. What sorts of contradictions? You'd prefer not to compete with your good friend at work. But your work is a zero-sum game and only one of you can win. How are you to choose between alienating a friend and putting food on the table?

71. We are even confused about right and wrong. We would prefer to act ethically rather than immorally, unless that preference has been trained out of us, but our

personal righteousness seems to hang by a thread that breaks too easily and too often.

72. We do not always do the right thing or even want to do the right thing. And we know that it's on our shoulders to deal with such moral shortfalls. There is no one else to blame, no one else to consult, and no one who can magically make us ethical.

73. We understand that our ethics do not come from on high. The universe is not conscious in some "soulful" way and there are no cosmic purposes, cosmic unity, or cosmic considerations. Individually and collectively, either we do good or we don't.

74. We live in a maelstrom of contradictions. It would be easy to throw up our hands and cry, "Too much!" But it doesn't appear to be too much. Yes, it is too much for many people and for all people some of the time. But we can weather our nature.

75. Indeed, we are stuck, badly stuck. But we have been built with the invaluable ability to stand to one side of the storm, even though the storm is raging within us, and create stillness and calmness. You have been built with that game- changing ability.

76. This is life. We see it, acknowledge our struggles, and try not to blink. We stand off to one side, in the stillness of self-created silence, hoping to make sense of it all. We forthrightly own our confusions and our contradictions and we laugh a little.

77. Our circumstances may doom us, as when our plane goes down in the open ocean. But our human nature need not doom us. Acknowledging the struggles that come with

human nature is not the same as being defeated by those pressing struggles.

78. Despite the contradictions and confusions that come with the territory of being human, we can coax meaning into existence, maybe even enough meaning to allow life to feel meaningful a good deal of the time.

79. Despite those contradictions and confusions, we can decide what's important to us, call those choices our life purpose choices, and live those life purpose choices for portions of each day, even on those cloudy days full of errands and nothingness.

80. Despite those contradictions and confusions, which make an awful noise, we can practice stillness and achieve an inner quiet that allows us to manifest our potential, make our wisest decisions, and meet our self-obligations.

81. There is a material world. When you cut your finger, you will bleed. But there is also an inner world, animated by consciousness and flavored by our style of in-dwelling, where we can imagine ourselves bleeding green and not red.

82. We can imagine, we can love, we can laugh, we can create things that are beautiful, good and true; and we can do all this even as we understand the powerful arguments for mistrusting words like truth, beauty and goodness.

83. We can have a philosophy of life that isn't wishful or ignorant. We can parlay our ideas about self-obligation, healthy in-dwelling, life purpose choosing, meaning coaxing, absurd rebellion, and our many other ideas into something rock solid.

84. We can have a philosophy of life that doesn't ignore,

deny or sugarcoat history. Are human divisions deeper than we would like to admit? Are human beings regularly cruel to one another and a danger to one another? History says yes to all that.

85. But history is also replete with victories of the human spirit, examples of genuine fellow feeling, and tales of heroism in the service of freedom and fairness. Those, too, are true. A kirist can look to those as proof of what is real and possible.

21

END NOTE

I hope you've enjoyed learning about kirism. Maybe you're even motivated to live as a kirist. If you do make that life decision, I would love to hear how it goes for you. Drop me a note to ericmaisel@hotmail.com and share your thoughts, your experiences, and your story.

I will continue to add kirism books to the kirist literature. You'll find future books at kirism.com, where you can also learn about volunteer opportunities and about how to donate to kirism. Donations will help us spread the word.

If you would like to interview me, if you would like me to speak to your group or organization, if you would like guidelines for running a kirism study group, if you have any questions, or if you'd like to get in touch with me for any reason, drop me a line to ericmaisel@hotmail.com. I look forward to hearing from you!

Printed in Great Britain
by Amazon